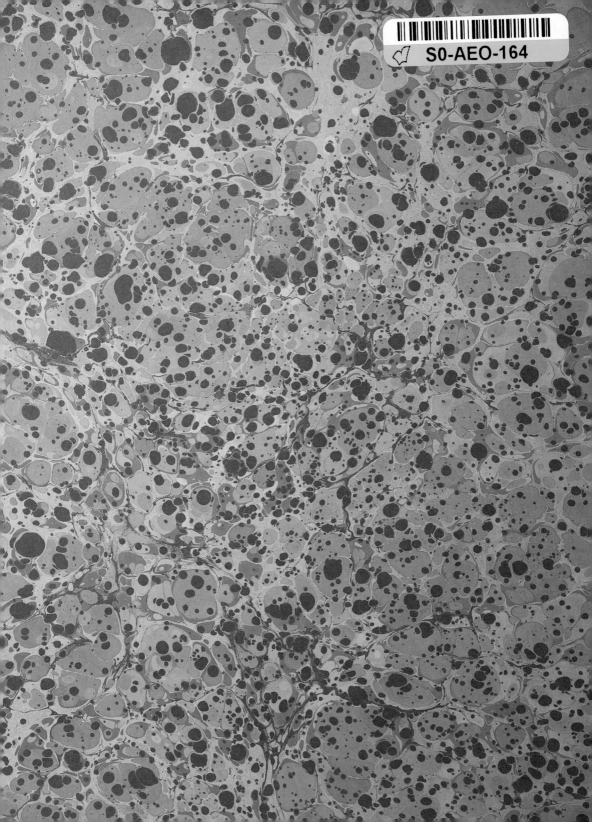

FLORENCE WELCH

USELESS MAGIC

CROWN
ARCHETYPE
NEW YORK

To my Mother
and Father

CONTENTS

I MAKE SONGS TO
TIE PEOPLE TO ME

WITH A RIBBON OF
FANTASY AROUND
THEIR NECKS

SUCH A BEAUTIFUL
BOW.

THAT I HOLD IN MY
FIST

AND I WILL NOT LET
GO.

PREFACE

Songs can be incredibly prophetic, like subconscious warnings or messages to myself, but I often don't know what I'm trying to say till years later. Or a prediction comes true and I couldn't do anything to stop it, so it seems like a kind of useless magic.

As if the song is somehow speaking through me in its own language. And I am a conduit but totally oblivious to its wisdom.

That's why poetry, or even having the lyrics written down somewhere, is strange for me. The act of singing gives the most mundane words and phrases reverence and glory. You can make a shrine out of anything. The song has its own personality, and is bigger and stronger than I am. With more to say, to just write something down and let it stay there, on the page, seems to me an enormously vulnerable thing. And that's why poetry has in many ways turned out more exposing.

I don't know what makes a song a song and a poem a poem: they have started to bleed into each other at this stage.

You can have everything.

Chateau Marmont
hollywood
CHAOS
MAGIC
8221 Sunset Boulevard Hollywood California 90046
Telephone (323) 656-1010 Facsimile (323) 655-5311

FLORENCE

LUNGS

DOG DAYS ARE OVER

Happiness hit her like a train on a track
Coming towards her, stuck still, no turning back
She hid around corners and she hid under beds
She killed it with kisses and from it she fled
With every bubble she sank with a drink
And washed it away down the kitchen sink

The dog days are over
The dog days are done
The horses are coming so you better run

Run fast for your mother run fast for your father
Run for your children for your sisters and brothers
Leave all your love and your longing behind
You can't carry it with you if you want to survive

The dog days are over
The dog days are done
Can't you hear the horses
'Cause here they come

And I never wanted anything from you
Except everything you had
And what was left after that too

Happiness hit her like a bullet in the back
Struck from a great height
By someone who should have known better than that

The dog days are over
The dog days are done
Can you hear the horses
'Cause here they come

Run fast for your mother run fast for your father
Run for your children for your sisters and brothers
Leave all your love and your longing behind
You can't carry it with you if you want to survive

The dog days are over
The dog days are done
Can you hear the horses
'Cause here they come

The dog days are over
The dog days are done
The horses are coming
So you better run

The dog days are over
The dog days are done
The horses are coming
So you better run

GLASTONBURY.

max
80.40
mins.

Birdsong.

Coffin Song.

~~falling~~

Ghosts

Girl with one eye

~~falling~~.

hospital beds.

~~Brick~~ Lungs

Bricks

Donkey Kosh

Kiss with a fist

Dog Dayz.

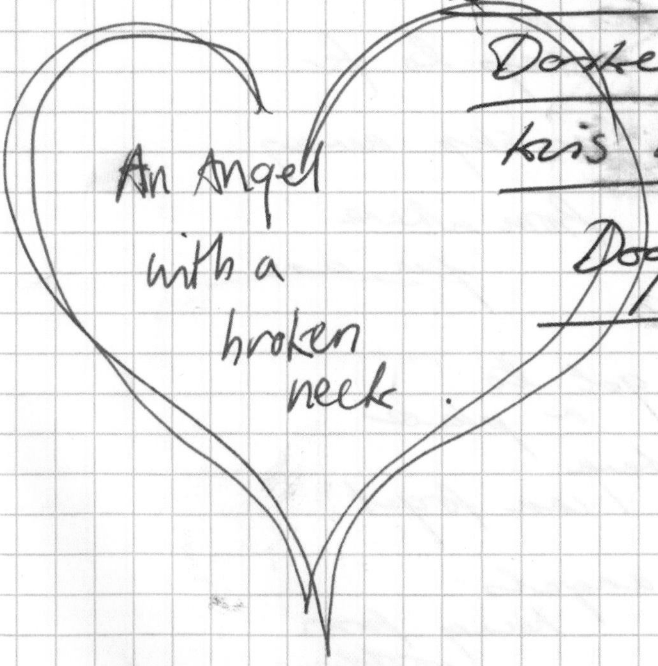
An Angel
with a
broken
neck.

I feel super dizzy
on the first day of the
tour.
My head is going to fall
off.

Ghe

I feel super super dizzy
its the first day of the
tour.
my head is going to fall
off.

24. 9. 09. x
NEWCASTL E ♡

ITTER.
taught
how to
to
e to
what
ead.
ica
e I bel
your lit
from ele
ica
follow

RABBIT HEART

The looking glass so shiny and new
How quickly the glamour fades
I start spinning slipping out of time
Was that the wrong pill to take
You made a deal and now it seems you have to offer up
But will it ever be enough
It's not enough

Here I am a rabbit hearted girl
Frozen in the headlights
It seems I made the final sacrifice

We raise it up, this offering
We raise it up

This is a gift, it comes with a price
Who is the lamb and who is the knife?
Midas is king and he holds me so tight
Turns me to gold in the sunlight

I look around but I can't find you
If only I could see your face
I start rushing towards the skyline
I wish that I could just be brave

I must become a lion hearted girl
Ready for a fight
Before I make the final sacrifice

We raise it up, this offering
We raise it up
This is a gift, it comes with a price
Who is the lamb and who is the knife?
Midas is king and he holds me so tight
And turns me to gold in the sunlight

Raise it up, raise it up
Raise it up, raise it up

And in the spring I shed my skin
And it blows away with the changing winds
The waters turn from blue to red
As towards the sky I offer it

This is a gift, it comes with a price
Who is the lamb and who is the knife?
Midas is king and he holds me so tight
And turns me to gold in the sunlight

This is a gift, it comes with a price
Who is the lamb and who is the knife?
Midas is king and he holds me so tight
And turns me to gold in the sunlight

This is a gift, it comes with a price
Who is the lamb and who is the knife?
Midas is king and he holds me so tight
And turns me to gold in the sunlight
This is a gift

I'M NOT CALLING YOU A LIAR

I'm not calling you a liar
Just don't lie to me
I'm not calling you a thief
Just don't steal from me
I'm not calling you a ghost
Just stop haunting me
And I love you so much
I'm gonna let you
Kill me

There's a ghost in my lungs
And it sighs in my sleep
Wraps itself around my tongue
As it softly speaks
Then it walks, then it walks with my legs

To fall, to fall
To fall, at your feet
Oh but for the grace of God go on
And when you kiss me, I'm happy enough to die

I'm not calling you a liar
Just don't lie to me
And I love you so much
I'm gonna let you
I'm not calling you a thief
Just don't
And I love you so much
I'm gonna let you
Oh, I'm not calling you a ghost
Just don't

There's a ghost in my mouth
And it talks in my sleep
Wraps itself around my tongue
As it softly speaks
Then it walks, then it walks
Then it walks with my legs

To fall, to fall, to fall, to fall, to fall, to fall
To fall, to fall, to fall, to fall
To fall, at your feet
Oh but for the grace of God go on
And when you kiss me, I'm happy enough

I AINT NEVER SCARED

because

I' aint never been scared.

Im sorry if you
couldn't find
me
I have been
in the
woods.
I put myself
there because
I couldn't be good.
I have been
running with
foxes and
hunting with
crows.
and I have
found myself
a home
where no body goes.

HOWL

If you could only see the beast you've made of me
I held it in but now it seems you've set it running free
Screaming in the dark, I howl when we're apart
Drag my teeth across your chest to taste your beating heart

My fingers claw your skin, try to tear my way in
You are the moon that breaks the night for which I have to howl
My fingers claw your skin, try to tear my way in
You are the moon that breaks the night for which I have to

Howl, howl, howl, howl

Now there's no holding back, I'm ready to attack
My blood is singing with your voice, I want to pour it out
The saints can't help me now, the ropes have been unbound
I hunt for you with bloodied feet across the hallowed ground

Like some child possessed, the beast howls in my veins
I want to find you, tear out all of your tenderness

And howl, howl, howl, howl

Be careful of the curse that falls on young lovers
Starts so soft and sweet and turns them to hunters
Hunters, hunters, hunters
Hunters, hunters, hunters

The fabric of your flesh, pure as a wedding dress
Until I wrap myself inside your arms I cannot rest
The saints can't help me now, the ropes have been unbound
I hunt for you with bloodied feet across the hallowed ground
And howl

Be careful of the curse that falls on young lovers
Starts so soft and sweet and turns them to hunters

A man who's pure of heart and says his prayers by night
May still become a wolf when the autumn moon is bright

If you could only see the beast you've made of me
I held it in but now it seems you've set it running free
The saints can't help me now, the ropes have been unbound
I hunt for you with bloodied feet across the hallowed ground

You have Slain me...

have merry
on usual

you hit me
once i'll hit
you back
you gave a kick
I gave a slap
you smashed a plate
over my head
then I set fire to
our bed x 2

pto →

KISS WITH A FIST

You hit me once
I hit you back
You gave a kick
I gave a slap
You smashed a plate over my head
Then I set fire to our bed

You hit me once
I hit you back
You gave a kick
I gave a slap
You smashed a plate over my head
Then I set fire to our bed, oh

My black eye casts no shadow
Your red eye sees no shame
Your slap don't stick
Your kicks don't hit
So we remain the same
Love sticks
Sweat drips
Break the lock if it don't fit

A kick to the teeth is good for some
A kiss with a fist is better than none
A kiss with a fist is better than none

I broke your jaw once before
I spilled your blood upon the floor
You broke my leg in return
So sit back and watch the bed burn
Love sticks
Sweat drips
Break the lock if it don't fit

A kick in the teeth is good for some
A kiss with a fist is better than none, oh
A kiss with a fist is better than none

You hit me once
I hit you back
You gave a kick
I gave a slap
You smashed a plate over my head
Then I set fire to our bed, oh

You hit me once
I hit you back
You gave a kick
I gave a slap
You smashed a plate over my head
Then I set fire to our bed

favorite songs.

Not over Yet - klaxons

Babooshka - Kate Bush

LIBERTINE - Patrick Wolf,

Ramalama Bang - Roisin Murphy
Bang

Hoist that Rag - Tom Waits,

~~LEAN TEEN - White denim~~

KIDS - MGMT

WALKING ON BROKEN GLASS - ~~Annie~~ Lennox.

CHANGE GONNA COME - SAM COOKE.

WADE IN THE WATER - EVA CASSIDY.

ELEPHANT GUN - BEIRUT.

Bon IVER - CREATURE FIT.

Dont just Do something - spiritualized

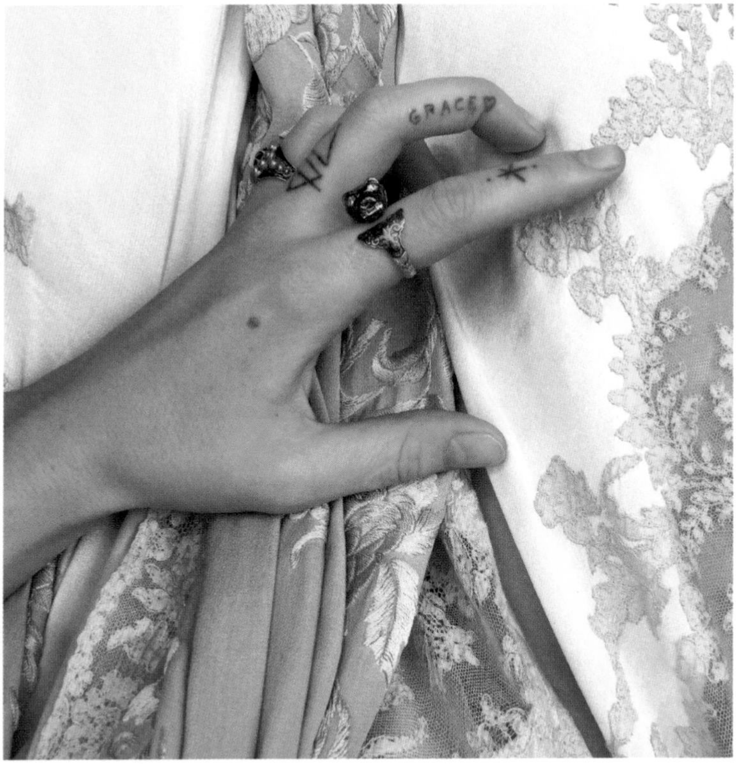
GRACED

this is a song for
my sister.

~~etc~~

Grace

read
softly
when
you go
because
~~where~~
where
you
go you
take
my heart
I hold it
in your
pocket
before we
were
apart.

here is a
song to
keep
you safe
you can wear it
and
your ~~ext~~
neck
~~or~~
~~to~~ ~~feel~~ it
to your
ankle
so wherever
you
walk you
won't
forget.

~~keep my heart in your~~
~~pocket~~
~~and take it with~~
you

DRUMMING SONG

There's a drumming noise inside my head
That starts when you're around
I swear that you could hear it
It makes such an almighty sound

There's a drumming noise inside my head
That throws me to the ground
I swear that you should hear it
It makes such an almighty sound

Louder than sirens
Louder than bells
Sweeter than heaven
And harder than hell

I ran to the tower when the church bells chimed
I hoped that they would clear my mind
They left a ringing in my ear
But that drum's still beating loud and clear

Louder than sirens
Louder than bells
Sweeter than heaven
And harder than hell

Louder than sirens
Louder than bells
Sweeter than heaven
And harder than hell

Louder than sirens
Louder than bells
Sweeter than heaven
And harder than hell

As I move my feet towards your body
I can hear this beat, it fills my head up
And gets louder and louder
It fills my head up and gets louder and louder
I run to the river and dive straight in
I pray that the water will drown out the din
But as the water fills my mouth
It couldn't wash the echoes out
But as the water fills my mouth
It couldn't wash the echoes out

I swallow the sound and it swallows me whole
'Till there's nothing left inside my soul
I'm as empty as that beating drum
But the sound has just begun

As I move my feet towards your body
I can hear this beat, it fills my head up
And gets louder and louder
It fills my head up and gets louder and louder

There's a drumming noise inside my head
That starts when you're around
I swear that you could hear it
It makes such an almighty sound

There's a drumming noise inside my head
That starts when you're around
I swear that you could hear it
It makes such an almighty sound

Louder than sirens
Louder than bells
Sweeter than heaven
And harder than hell

Louder than sirens
Louder than bells
Sweeter than heaven
And harder than hell

As I move my feet towards your body
I can hear this beat, it fills my head up
And gets louder and louder
It fills my head up and gets louder and louder

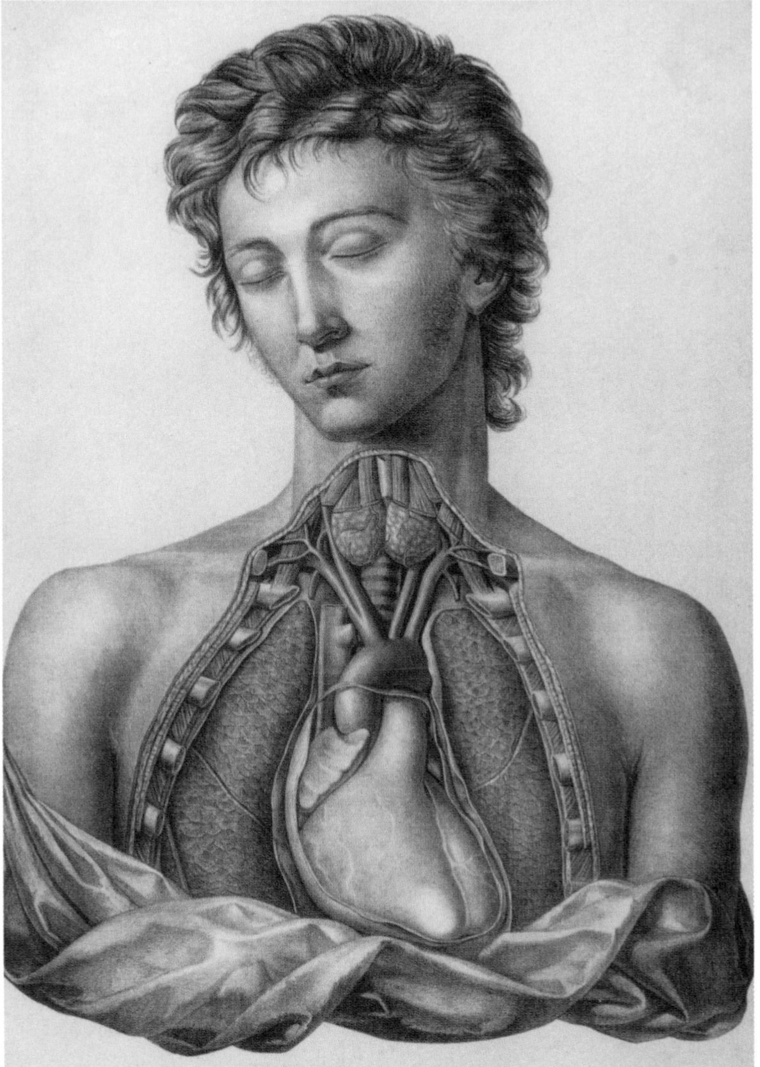

FRIDERICI TIEDEMANN TABULAE ARTERIARUM.

BETWEEN TWO LUNGS

Between two lungs
It was released
The breath that carried me
The sigh that blew me forward

'Cause it was trapped
Trapped between two lungs
It was trapped between two lungs
It was trapped between two lungs

And my running feet could fly
Each breath screaming
'We are all too young to die'

Between two lungs
It was released
The breath that passed from you to me
That flew between us as we slept
That slipped from your mouth into mine
It crept between two lungs
It was released

The breath that passed from you to me
That flew between us as we slept
That slipped from your mouth into mine
It crept
'Cause it was trapped
Trapped between two lungs
It was trapped between two lungs

Gone are the days of begging
The days of theft
No more gasping for a breath
The air has filled me head-to-toe
And I can see the ground far below
I have this breath
And I hold it tight
And I keep it in my chest
With all my might
I pray to God this breath will last
As it pushes past my lips
As I gasp

COSMIC LOVE

A falling star fell from your heart and landed in my eyes
I screamed aloud, as it tore through them, and now it's left me blind

The stars, the moon, they have all been blown out
You left me in the dark
No dawn, no day, I'm always in this twilight
In the shadow of your heart

And in the dark, I can hear your heartbeat
I tried to find the sound
But then it stopped, and I was in the darkness
So darkness I became

The stars, the moon, they have all been blown out
You left me in the dark
No dawn, no day, I'm always in this twilight
In the shadow of your heart

I took the stars from our eyes, and then I made a map
And knew that somehow I could find my way back
Then I heard your heart beating, you were in the darkness too
So I stayed in the darkness with you

The stars, the moon, they have all been blown out
You left me in the dark
No dawn, no day, I'm always in this twilight
In the shadow of your heart

The stars, the moon, they have all been blown out
You left me in the dark
No dawn, no day, I'm always in this twilight
In the shadow of your heart

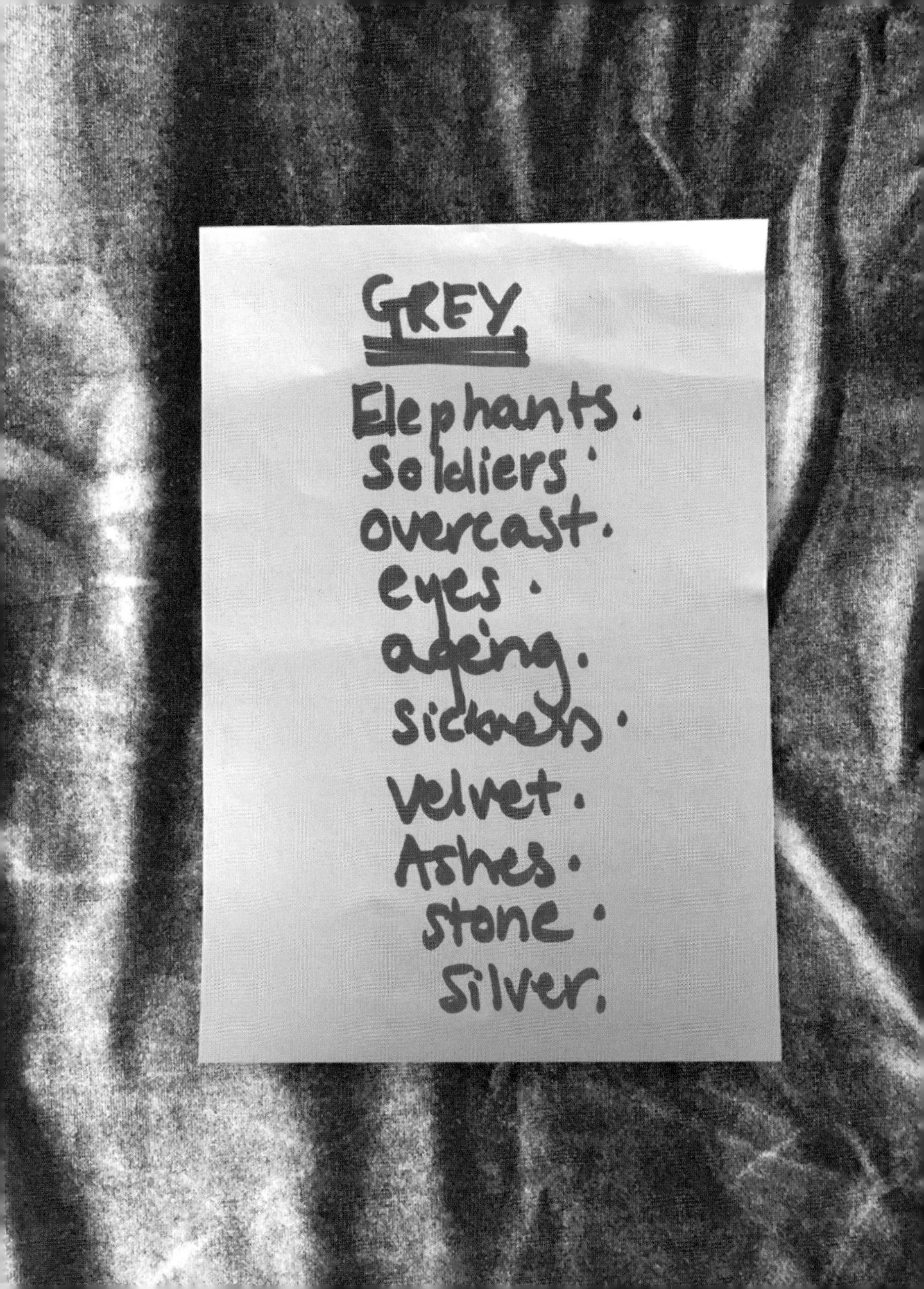
GREY
Elephants.
Soldiers.
overcast.
eyes.
ageing.
Sickness.
Velvet.
Ashes.
stone.
Silver.

drifting

~~mocking~~

~~forwarded~~

~~I can't wait for that day~~ ?

lights out -

His heart stopped as she said ~~his~~ her name.

~~to die~~

I love you she said

he replied

'thats a shame'

So ~~sorry~~ that you feel that ~~wrong~~.

We got
ready to
go out,

the excitement
a fireworks in my
mouth.

I DONT
WANT
ANYTHING
NOW OR
EVER
AGAIN -

MY BOY BUILDS COFFINS

My boy builds coffins with hammers and nails
He doesn't build ships, he has no use for sails
He doesn't make tables, dressers or chairs
He can't carve a whistle, 'cause he just doesn't care

My boy builds coffins for the rich and the poor
Kings and queens, they've all knocked on his door
Beggars and liars, gypsies and thieves
They all come to him 'cause he's so eager to please

My boy builds coffins he makes them all day
But it's not just for work and it isn't for play
He's made one for himself
One for me too
One of these days he'll make one for you
For you, for you, for you

My boy builds coffins for better or worse
Some say it's a blessing, some say it's a curse
He fits them together in sunshine or rain
Each one is unique, no two are the same

My boy builds coffins and I think it's a shame
That when each one's been made, he can't see it again
He crafts every one with love and with care
Then it's thrown in the ground, it just isn't fair

My boy builds coffins he makes them all day
But it's not just for work and it isn't for play
He's made one for himself
One for me too
One of these days he'll make one for you
For you, for you, for you

HURRICANE DRUNK

No walls can keep me protected
No sleep
Nothing in between me and the rain
And you can't save me now
I'm in the grip of a hurricane
I'm gonna blow myself away

I'm going out
I'm gonna drink myself to death
And in the crowd
I see you with someone else
I brace myself
'Cause I know it's going to hurt
But I like to think, at least things can't get any worse

No hope
Don't want shelter
No calm
Nothing to keep me from the storm
And you can't hold me down
'Cause I belong to the hurricane
It's going to blow this all away

I'm going out
I'm gonna drink myself to death
And in the crowd
I see you with someone else
I brace myself
'Cause I know it's going to hurt
But I like to think at least things can't get any worse

I hope that you see me
'Cause I'm staring at you
But when you look over
You look right through
Then you lean and kiss her on the head
And I never felt so alive
And so dead

I'm going out
I'm gonna drink myself to death
And in the crowd
I see you with someone else
I brace myself
'Cause I know it's going to hurt
I'm going out

I'm going out
I'm gonna drink myself to death
And in the crowd
I see you with someone else
I brace myself
'Cause I know it's going to hurt

I'm going out
I'm going out
I'm going out
I'm going out
I'm going out
I'm going out

SO MUCH
BEAUTY
TO
BEHOLD

BLINDING

Seems that I have been held, in some dreaming state
A tourist in the waking world, never quite awake
No kiss, no gentle word could wake me from this slumber
Until I realize that it was you who held me under

Felt it in my fist, in my feet, in the hollows of my eyelids
Shaking through my skull, through my spine and down through my ribs

No more dreaming of the dead as if death itself was undone
No more calling like a crow for a boy, for a body in the garden
No more dreaming like a girl so in love, so in love
No more dreaming like a girl so in love, so in love
No more dreaming like a girl so in love with the wrong world

And I could hear the thunder and see the lightning crack
And all around the world was waking, I never could go back
'Cause all the walls of dreaming, they were torn right open
And finally it seemed that the spell was broken

And all my bones began to shake, my eyes flew open
And all my bones began to shake, my eyes flew open
No more dreaming of the dead as if death itself was undone
No more calling like a crow for a boy, for a body in the garden

No more dreaming like a girl so in love, so in love
No more dreaming like a girl so in love, so in love
No more dreaming like a girl so in love with the wrong world
Snow White's stitching up the circuit boards
Synapses slipping through the hidden door
Snow White's stitching up your circuit board

No more dreaming of the dead as if death itself was undone
No more calling like a crow for a boy, for a body in the garden
No more dreaming like a girl so in love, so in love
No more dreaming like a girl so in love, so in love
No more dreaming like a girl so in love with the wrong world

Snow White's stitching up the circuit boards
Synapses slipping through the hidden door
Snow White's stitching up your circuit board
Synapses slipping through the hidden door

2 knives in a gift box

good

- he will remember how much he likes you
- [redacted] will be there
  would be nice to see him
- maybe it would be good rebuild some bridges.
  head on the way to being friends.

Bad.

- It could be very awkward.
- he's working can't talk
- She could be there.
- you could remember how much you like him, and you can't have him.
- Do you want to be his friend?

So I didn't even go in the end.

It's a good thing

SWIMMING

Your songs remind me of swimming
Which I forgot when I started to sink
Dragged further away from the shore
And deeper into the drink

Sat on the bottom of the ocean
A stern and stubborn rock
'Cause your songs remind me of swimming
But somehow I forgot

I was sinking, and now I'm sunk
I was drinking, and now I'm drunk
Your songs remind me of swimming
But somehow I forgot

I tried to remember the chorus
I can't remember the verse
'Cause that song that sent me swimming
Is now the life jacket that burst

Rotting like a wreck on the ocean floor
Sinking like a siren that can't swim anymore
'Cause your songs remind me of swimming
But I can't swim anymore

Pull me out the water, cold and blue
I open my eyes and I see that it's you
So I dive straight back in the ocean
So I dive straight back in the ocean

Take a deep breath, suck the water in my chest
Take a deep breath, suck the water in my chest
Cross my fingers and hope for the best

Then all of a sudden, I heard a note
It started in my chest and ended in my throat
Then I realized, then I realized, then I realized
I was swimming
Yes, I was swimming
And now I'm swimming
Yes, I am swimming

Your songs remind me of swimming
Which I forgot when I started to sink
Your songs remind me of swimming
Which I forgot when I started to sink
Oh, your songs remind me of swimming
Which I forgot when I started
Your songs remind me of swimming
Which I forgot when I started to sink

a quivering mess of
blood and
bones.
~~thrown from~~

Im awake in the world
and not
for the
first time

IM IN LOVE
I have opened my
WITH THE WORLD.
eyes
and I
see
that
its mine

NOW I WANT
what do you want to happen
~~do you think~~
TO GO
~~that~~
~~it cannot~~?

you can
make it yourself.

I made my own universe
I dont need
you to

SWIMMING.

THERE'S BEAUTY IN
~~THE BROKEN~~

like end of an ugly Beggining

misery guts.

spilling my guts.

what
can I do
with
this life of
mine
that
is yours
to hold
its intertwined

FALLING

I've fallen out of favour
And I've fallen from grace
Fallen out of trees
And I've fallen on my face
Fallen out of taxis
Out of windows too
Fell in your opinion
When I fell in love with you

Sometimes I wish for falling
Wish for the release
Wish for falling through the air
To give me some relief
Because falling's not the problem
When I'm falling I'm at peace
It's only when I hit the ground
It causes all the grief

This is a song for a scribbled-out name
And my love keeps writing again and again
This is a song for a scribbled-out name
And my love keeps writing again and again

I'll dance myself up
Drunk myself down
Find people to love
Left people to drown
I'm not scared to jump
I'm not scared to fall
If there was nowhere to land
I wouldn't be scared
At all

Sometimes I wish for falling
Wish for the release
Wish for falling through the air
To give me some relief
Because falling's not the problem
When I'm falling I'm at peace
It's only when I hit the ground
It causes all the grief

I CANT
LISTEN
TO MUSI
ANYMORE
FLORENCE AND THE MACHINE

The AMAZING SELF DESTRUCTO GIRL.

SHE'S NOT HERE
TO SAVE THE WORLD
IF THERE'S A
BAD DECISION
TO BE MADE
YOU CAN BE SURE
SHE'll MAKE IT!
IF THERES A PROMISE
TO BE KEPT,
YOU CAN BE SURE
SHE'll BREAK IT.

ARE YOU HURTING THE ONE YOU LOVE?

Are you hurting the one you love?
You say you've found heaven but you can't find God
Are you hurting the one you love?
Bite your tongue till it tastes like blood

Are you hurting the one you love?
So many glasses on the table top
Are you hurting the one you love?
You'd like to stay in heaven but the rules are too tough

Tough
It's just too tough
Tough
It's just too tough

Are you hurting the one you love?
When they watched the walls and the ticking clock
Are you hurting the one you love?
And was it something you could not stop?

Could not stop
Stop
Could not stop
Stop
Could not stop
Stop
Could not stop
Stop
Could not stop

Are you hurting the one you love?
When you leave them sleeping in the middle of the floor
Are you hurting the one you love?

Are you hurting the one you love?
And if heaven knows then who will stop?
Are you hurting the one you love?
You said you got to heaven, but it wasn't enough

were not out of the woods just yet

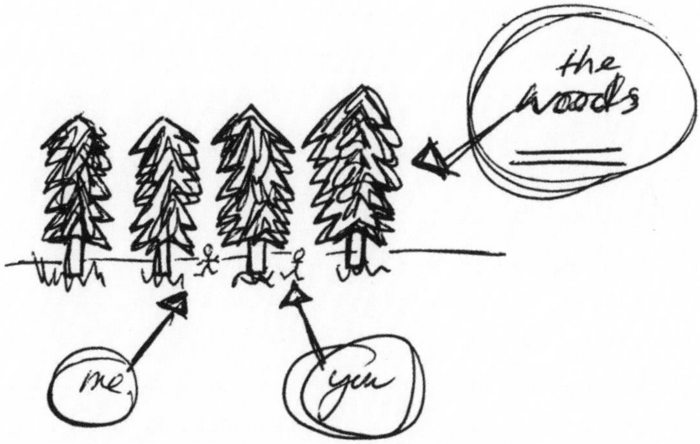

GET SOME
SOUL [redacted]

WEW

FLOZWALD
THE FEARFULL

I AINT
NEVER
SCARED

IZLWAD THE UNSTEADY..

BIRD SONG

Well I didn't tell anyone, but a bird flew by
Saw what I'd done, he set up a nest outside
And he sang about what I'd become
He sang so loud, sang so clear
I was afraid all the neighbours would hear
So I invited him in, just to reason with him
I promised I wouldn't do it again

But he sang louder and louder inside the house
And no I couldn't get him out
So I trapped him under a cardboard box
Stood on it to make him stop
I picked up the bird and above the din I said
'That's the last song you'll ever sing'
Held him down, broke his neck
Taught him a lesson he wouldn't forget

But in my dreams began to creep
That old familiar tweet tweet tweet

I opened my mouth to scream and shout
I waved my arms and flapped about
But I couldn't scream, and I couldn't shout
Couldn't scream and I couldn't shout

I opened my mouth to scream and shout
Waved my arms and flapped about
But I couldn't scream, I couldn't shout
The song was coming from my mouth
From my mouth

I am half a bird
half a girl.
you are half of
me and
I am all for you

CEREMONIALS

ONLY IF FOR A NIGHT

And I had a dream
About my old school
And she was there all pink and gold and glittering
I threw my arms around her legs
Came to weeping, came to weeping
Came to weeping, came to weeping

And I heard your voice
As clear as day
And you told me I should concentrate
It was all so strange
And so surreal
That a ghost should be
So practical
Only if for a night

And the only solution was to stand and fight
And my body was bruised and I was set alight
But you came over me like some holy rite
And although I was burning, you're the only light
Only if for a night

And the grass was so green against my new clothes
And I did cartwheels in your honour
Dancing on tiptoes
My own secret ceremonials
Before the service began
In the graveyard doing handstands

And I heard your voice
As clear as day
And you told me I should concentrate
It was all so strange
And so surreal
That a ghost should be
So practical
Only if for a night

And the only solution was to stand and fight
And my body was bruised and I was set alight
But you came over me like some holy rite
And although I was burning, you're the only light
Only if for a night

My doe, my dear, my darling
Tell me what all this sighing's about
Tell me what all this sighing's about

And I heard your voice
As clear as day
And you told me I should concentrate
It was all so strange
And so surreal
That a ghost should be
So practical
Only if for a night
Only if for a night

AND 

ALTHOUGH

I WAS

BURNING

YOUR THE

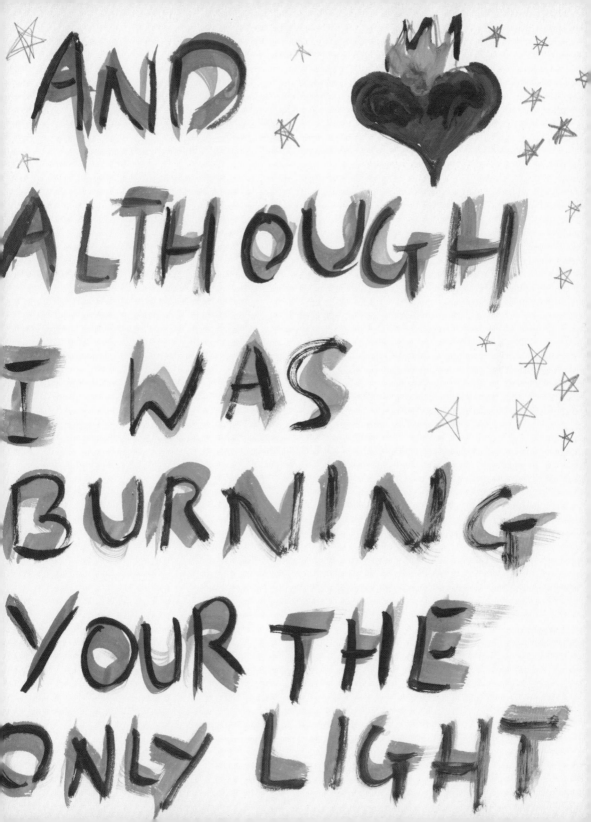

ONLY LIGHT

talk to me
sometime
anytime.

Things to do
today

go to tate modern.
buy. Reel gone
Kate Bush.
go to Fop. Drums not Dead.

go to Primemark.

cycle to that
place
with the
sights.
take polaroid. →
get polaroid

NO ONE

IS NOT

LOVED

YEAH

YEAH

YIPPIE

YIPPIE

YEAH

SHAKE IT OUT

Regrets collect like old friends
Here to relive your darkest moments
I can see no way, I can see no way
And all of the ghouls come out to play

And every demon wants his pound of flesh
But I like to keep some things to myself
I like to keep my issues drawn
It's always darkest before the dawn

And I've been a fool and I've been blind
I can never leave the past behind
I can see no way, I can see no way
I'm always dragging that horse around

All of his questions, such a mournful sound
Tonight I'm gonna bury that horse in the ground
So I like to keep my issues drawn
But it's always darkest before the dawn

Shake it out, shake it out, shake it out, shake it out, ooh whoa
Shake it out, shake it out, shake it out, shake it out, ooh whoa
And it's hard to dance with a devil on your back
So shake him off, oh whoa

And I am done with my graceless heart
So tonight I'm gonna cut it out and then restart
'Cause I like to keep my issues drawn
It's always darkest before the dawn

Shake it out, shake it out, shake it out, shake it out, ooh whoa
Shake it out, shake it out, shake it out, shake it out, ooh whoa
And it's hard to dance with a devil on your back
So shake him off, oh whoa

And it's hard to dance with a devil on your back
And given half the chance would I take any of it back
It's a fine romance but it's left me so undone
It's always darkest before the dawn
Oh whoa, oh whoa . . .

And I'm damned if I do and I'm damned if I don't
So here's to drinks in the dark at the end of my rope
And I'm ready to suffer and I'm ready to hope
It's a shot in the dark aimed right at my throat
'Cause looking for heaven, found the devil in me
Looking for heaven, found the devil in me
Well what the hell I'm gonna let it happen to me, yeah

Shake it out, shake it out, shake it out, shake it out, ooh whoa
Shake it out, shake it out, shake it out, shake it out, ooh whoa
And it's hard to dance with a devil on your back
So shake him off, oh whoa

Shake it out, shake it out, shake it out, shake it out, ooh whoa
Shake it out, shake it out, shake it out, shake it out, ooh whoa
And it's hard to dance with a devil on your back
So shake him off, oh whoa

WHAT THE WATER GAVE ME

Time it took us
To where the water was
That's what the water gave me
And time goes quicker
Between the two of us
Oh, my love, don't forsake me
Take what the water gave me

Lay me down
Let the only sound
Be the overflow
Pockets full of stones

Lay me down
Let the only sound
Be the overflow

And oh, poor Atlas
The world's a beast of a burden
You've been holding up a long time
And all this longing
And the ships are left to rust
That's what the water gave us

So lay me down
Let the only sound
Be the overflow
Pockets full of stones
Lay me down
Let the only sound
Be the overflow

’Cause they took your loved ones
But returned them in exchange for you
But would you have it any other way?
Would you have it any other way?
You couldn’t have it any other way

’Cause she’s a cruel mistress
And a bargain must be made
But oh, my love, don’t forsake me
When I let the water take me

So, lay me down
Let the only sound
Be the overflow
Pockets full of stones

Lay me down
Let the only sound
Be the overflow

Lay me down
Let the only sound
Be the overflow
Pockets full of stones

Lay me down
Let the only sound
Be the overflow

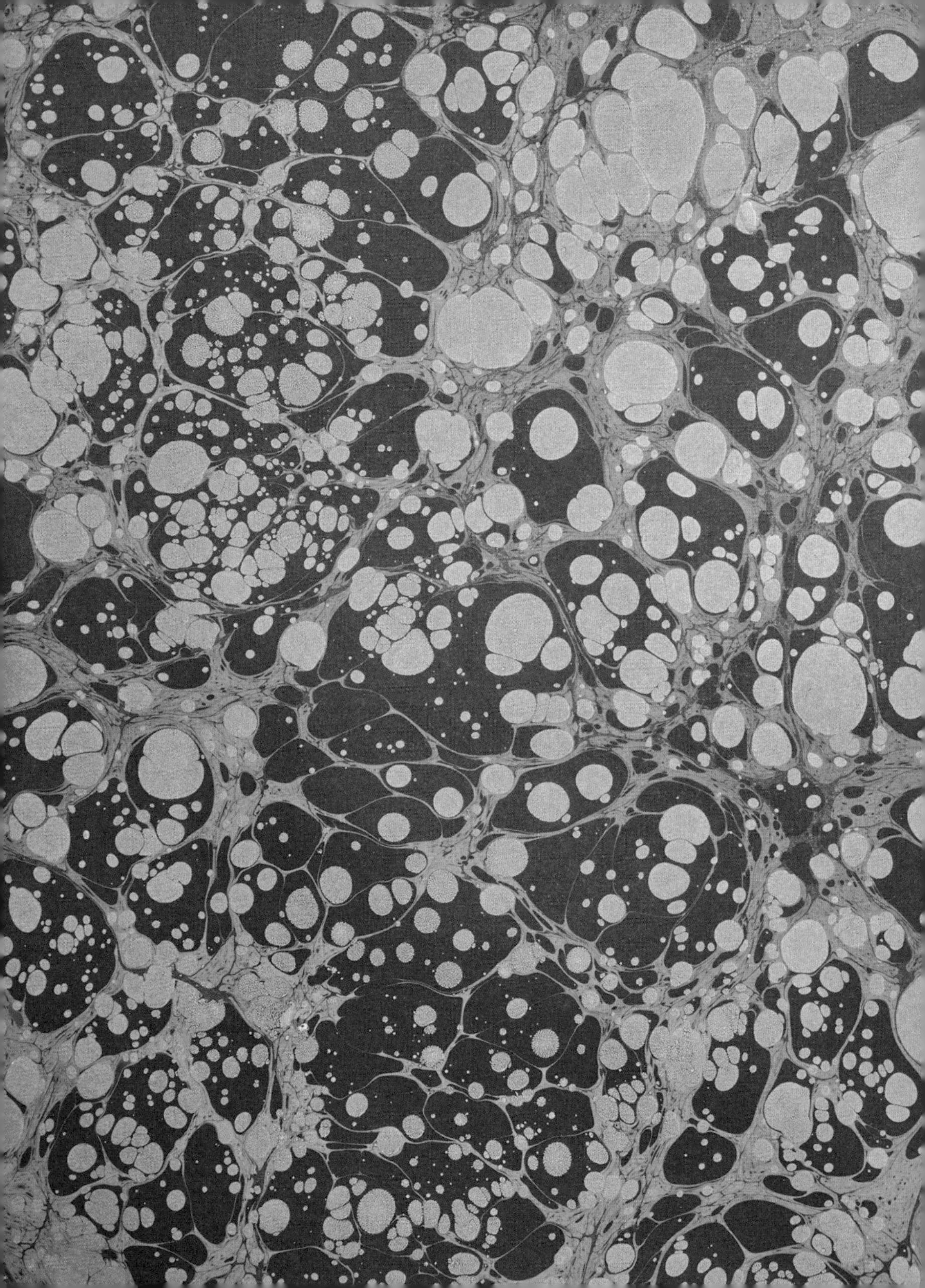

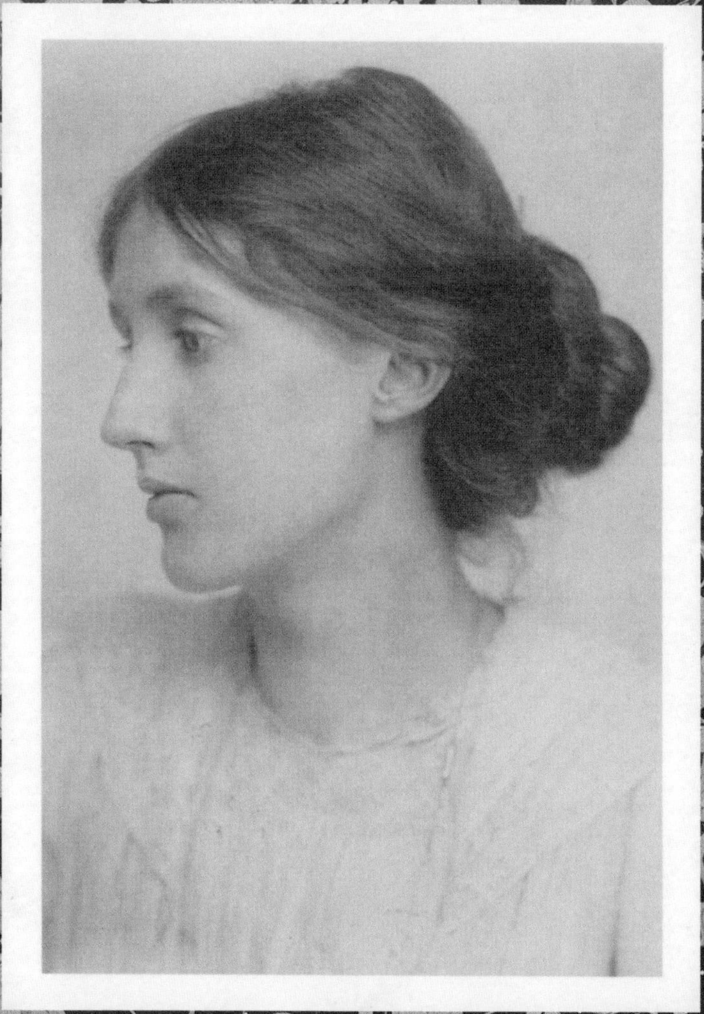

NEVER LET ME GO

Looking up from underneath
Fractured moonlight on the sea
Reflections still look the same to me
As before I went under

And it's peaceful in the deep
Cathedral where you cannot breathe
No need to pray, no need to speak
Now I am under all

Oh, and it's breaking over me
A thousand miles out to the seabed
Found the place to rest my head

Never let me go, never let me go
Never let me go, never let me go

And the arms of the ocean are carrying me
And all this devotion was rushing out of me
The crush is a heaven, for a sinner like me
But the arms of the ocean deliver me

Though the pressure's hard to take
It's the only way I can escape
It seems a heavy choice to make
But now I am under, oh

And it's breaking over me
A thousand miles down to the seabed
I found the place to rest my head
Never let me go, never let me go
Never let me go, never let me go

And the arms of the ocean are carrying me
So cold and so sweet
And all this devotion was rushing out of me

And the crush is a heaven, for a sinner like me
But the arms of the ocean deliver me

And it's over and I'm going under
But I'm not giving up
I'm just giving in

Oh, slipping underneath
So cold and so sweet

In the arms of the ocean, so sweet and so cold
And all this devotion, well, I never knew at all
The crush is a heaven, for a sinner like me
In the arms of the ocean, deliver me

Never let me go, never let me go
Never let me go, never let me go

Deliver me
Never let me go, never let me go
Never let me go, never let me go
Never let me go, never let me go

Deliver me
Never let me go, never let me go
Never let me go, never let me go

Deliver me
Never let me go, never let me go
And it's over
I'm going under
But I'm not giving up
I'm just giving in

Ah, slipping underneath
Oh, so cold, but so sweet

~~MY BODY~~

~~WAS SHOCKED~~

~~AND I FELL~~

~~TO THE~~

FLOOR.

~~IT WENT~~

~~INTO MY~~

~~ARM~~S

~~AND~~

~~I STARTE~~D

~~TO CRY~~

I WANTED TO SCREAM
AT ~~THE~~ BEAUTY OF
IT SCREAMING WITH
JOY ON AN EMPTY
~~STREET~~.

SOHO HOUSE
SOHO HOUSE
WEST HOLLYWOOD
WEST HOLLYWOOD

BREAKING DOWN

All along
It was always there you see
And even on my own
It was always standing next to me

I can see it coming from the edge of the room
Creeping in the streetlight
Holding my hand in the pale gloom
Can you see it coming now?

Oh, I think I'm breaking down again
Oh, I think I'm breaking down

All alone
Even when I was a child
I've always known
There was something to be frightened of

I can see you coming from the edge of the room
Creeping in the streetlight
Holding my hand in the pale gloom
Can you see it coming now?

Oh, I think I'm breaking down again
Oh, I think I'm breaking down

All alone
On the edge of sleep
My old familiar friend
Comes and lies down next to me
And I can see you coming from the edge of the room
Smiling in the streetlight
Even with my eyes shut tight
I still see him coming now

Oh, I think I'm breaking down again
Oh, I think I'm breaking down again
Oh, I think I'm breaking down again
Oh, I think I'm breaking down

There's no salvation
for me now
No space among the clouds
And I feel I'm heading
down

BUT THAT'S ALRIGHT

LOVER TO LOVER

I've been losin' sleep
I've been keepin' myself awake
I've been wandering the streets
For days and days and days

Road to road
Bed to bed
Lover to lover
And black to red
But I believe, I believe

There's no salvation for me now
No space among the clouds
And I've seen I'm heading down
That's alright, that's alright
That's alright, that's alright

And I've been taking chances
I've been setting myself up for the fall
And I've been keeping secrets
From my heart and from my soul

Going from road to road
Bed to bed
Lover to lover
Black to red
But I believe, I believe

There's no salvation for me now
No space among the clouds
And I feel that I'm heading down
But that's alright

That's alright
That's alright
That's alright

Road to road
Bed to bed
And lover to lover
And black to red
And road to road, bed to bed
And lover to lover

No space among the clouds
And I feel I'm heading down
But that's alright
That's alright

That's alright
That's alright
That's alright
That's alright

Road to road, bed to bed
And lover to lover
And black to red
And road to road, bed to bed

Lover to lover, to lover to lover
To lover to lover, to lover to lover
To lover to lover, to lover to lover

No salvation for me now
No salvation for me now
No salvation for me now
No salvation for me now

NO LIGHT, NO LIGHT

You are the hole in my head
You are the space in my bed
You are the silence in between
What I thought and what I said
You are the night-time fear
You are the morning when it's clear
When it's over you'll start
You're my head, you're my heart

No light, no light in your bright blue eyes
I never knew daylight could be so violent
A revelation in the light of day
You can't choose what stays and what fades away

And I'd do anything to make you stay
No light, no light
Tell me what you want me to say

Through the crowd I was crying out and
In your place there were a thousand other faces
I was disappearing in plain sight
Heaven help me I need to make it right

You want a revelation
You want to get it right
And it's a conversation
I just can't have tonight

You want a revelation
Some kind of resolution
You want a revelation

No light, no light in your bright blue eyes
I never knew daylight could be so violent
A revelation in the light of day
You can't choose what stays and what fades away
And I'd do anything to, to make you stay
No light, no light
Tell me what you want me to say

But would you leave me
If I told you what I've done
And would you leave me
If I told you what I've become

'Cause it's so easy
To say it to a crowd
But it's so hard, my love
To say it to you out loud

No light, no light in your bright blue eyes
I never knew daylight could be so violent
A revelation in the light of day
You can't choose what stays and what fades away

And I'd do anything to make you stay
No light, no light
Tell me what you want me to say

You want a revelation
You want to get it right
But it's a conversation
I just can't have tonight

You want a revelation
Some kind of resolution
You want a revelation

You want a revelation
You want to get it right
But it's a conversation
I just can't have tonight

You want a revelation
Some kind of resolution
Tell me what you want me to say

YOU CANT CHOOSE
WHAT STAYS
AND WHAT
FADES
AWAY

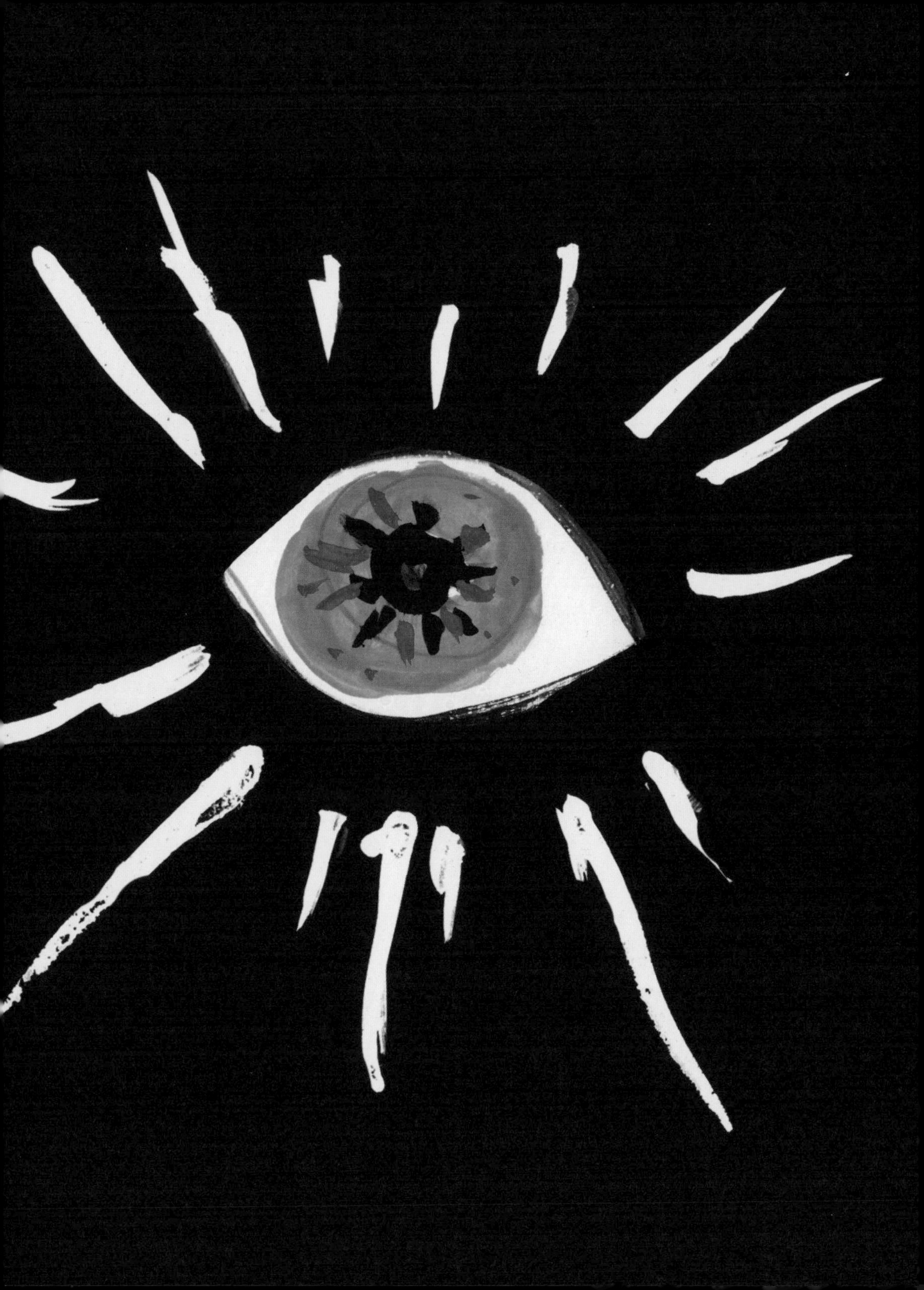

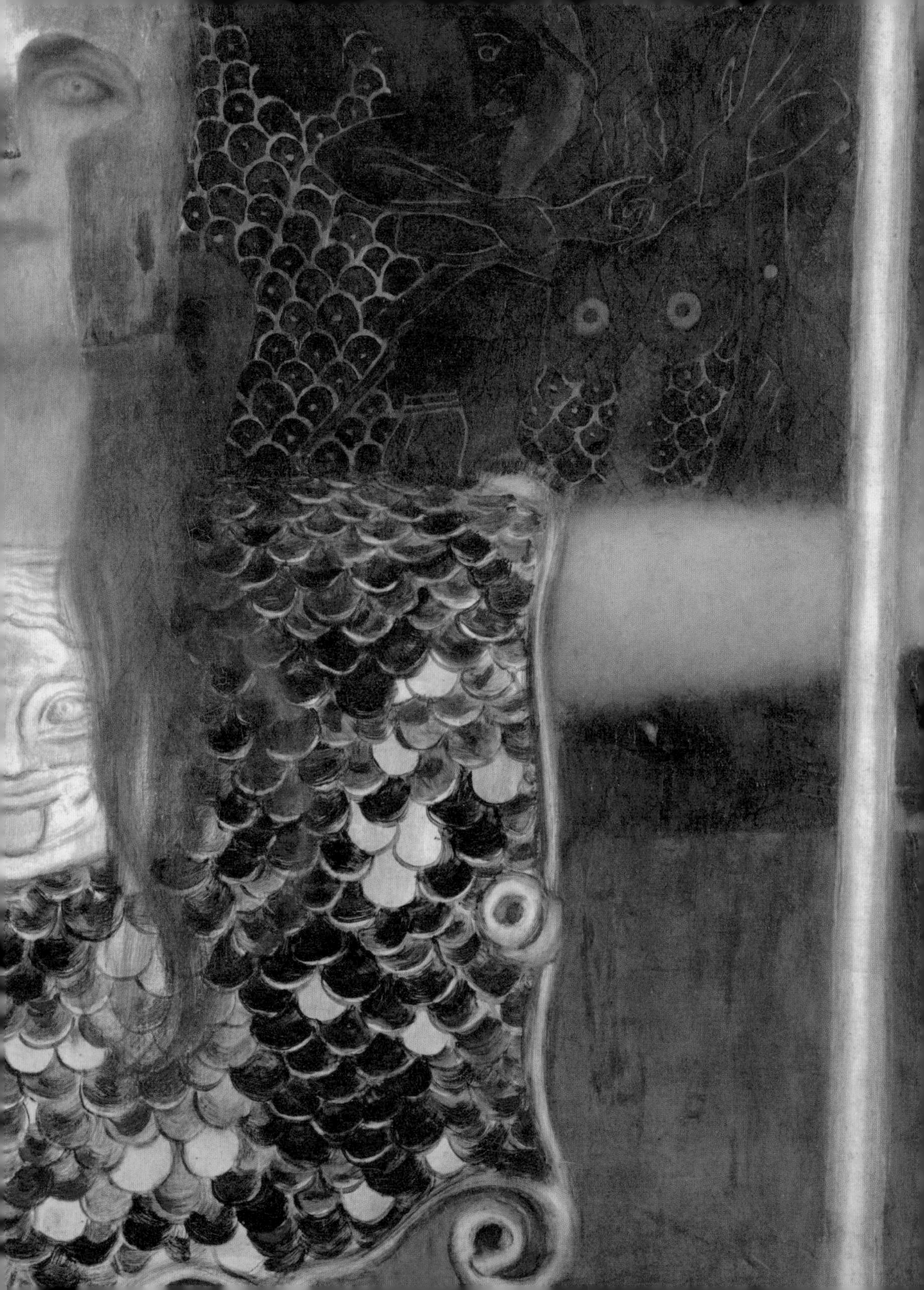

Sighing like a sleeper

Love like thunder

I burn I shiver.

I BURN

I'll keep all

~~or~~ your notes

and every note

that springs

from me

~~with.~~

SEVEN DEVILS

Holy water cannot help you now
Thousand armies couldn't keep me out
I don't want your money
I don't want your crown
See I've come to burn your kingdom down

Holy water cannot help you now
See I've come to burn your kingdom down
And no rivers and no lakes can put the fire out
I'm gonna raise the stakes, I'm gonna smoke you out

Seven devils all around me!
Seven devils in my house!
See they were there when I woke up this morning
I'll be dead before the day is done

Seven devils all around you
Seven devils in your house
See I was dead when I woke up this morning
I'll be dead before the day is done
Before the day is done

And now all your love will be exorcized
And we will find new saints to be canonized
It's an evensong
It's a litany
It's a battle cry
It's a symphony

Seven devils all around me
Seven devils in my house
See they were there when I woke up this morning
I'll be dead before the day is done

Seven devils all around you
Seven devils in your house
See I was dead when I woke up this morning
I'll be dead before the day is done
Before the day is done
Before the day is done
Before the day is done

You can't keep it out
It's coming through the walls
To devastate your heart
And to take your soul
For what has been done
Cannot be undone
In the eagle's eye
In the evensong

Seven devils all around you
Seven devils in your house
See I was dead when I woke up this morning
I'll be dead before the day is done
Before the day is done

BECOME A BEACON.

KEEP THAT FLAME ALIVE
THE FUTURE IS WITHIN YOU
IT BURNS BRIGHT IN YOUR HEART.

raise your love
hold it high
let it shine for miles and miles

you are not alone . . x

HEARTLINES

Oh the river, oh the river, it's running free
And oh the joy, oh the joy it brings to me
But I know it'll have to drown me
Before it can breathe easy

And I've seen it in the flights of birds
I've seen it in you, in the entrails of the animals
The blood running through, but in order to get to the heart of things
Sometimes you have to cut through

Keep it up
I know you can

Just keep following
The heartlines on your hand
Just keep following
The heartlines on your hand
Keep it up, I know you can
Just keep following
The heartlines on your hand
'Cause I am

Odyssey on odyssey and land over land
Creeping and crawling like the sea over sand
Still I follow heartlines on your hand

Just keep following the heartlines on your hand

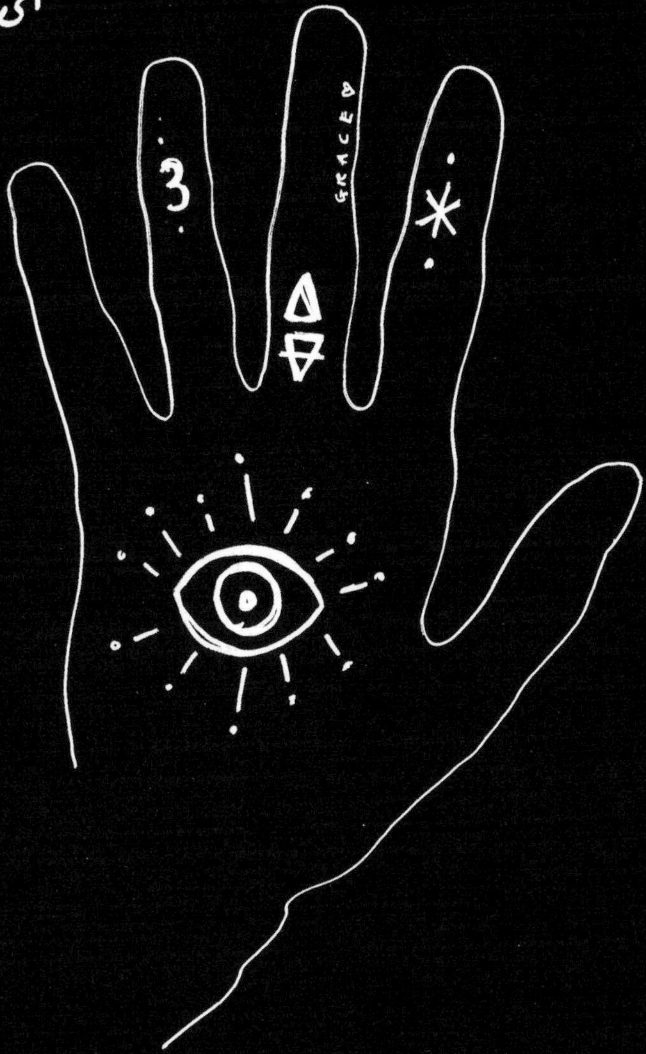

This fantasy, this fallacy, this tumbling stone
Echoes of a city that's long overgrown
Your heart is the only place that I call home
How can I be returned, you can
Keep it up, I know you can
Just keep following
The heartlines on your hand
Just keep following
The heartlines on your hand
Keep it up, I know you can
Just keep following
The heartlines on your hand

What a thing to do
What a thing to choose
But know, in some way, I'm there with you
Up against the wall
On a Wednesday afternoon
Just keep following
The heartlines on your hand
Just keep following
The heartlines on your hand
Keep it up, I know you can
Just keep following
The heartlines on your hand
'Cause I am

SPECTRUM

When we first came here
We were cold and we were clear
With no colours in our skin
We were light and paper-thin

And when we first came here
We were cold and we were clear
With no colours in our skin
'Till we let the spectrum in

Say my name
And every colour illuminates
We are shining
And we will never be afraid again

Say my name
As every colour illuminates
We are shining
And we will never be afraid again

Say my name
As every colour illuminates
We are shining
And we will never be afraid again

And when we come for you
We'll be dressed up all in blue
With the ocean in our arms
Kiss your eyes and kiss your palms

And when it's time to pray
We'll be dressed up all in grey
With metal on our tongues
And silver in our lungs

Say my name
And every colour illuminates
We are shining
And we will never be afraid again

Say my name
As every colour illuminates
We are shining
And we will never be afraid again

Say my name
As every colour illuminates
We are shining
And we will never be afraid again

And when we come back we'll be dressed in black
And you'll scream my name aloud
And we won't eat and we won't sleep
We'll drag bodies from the ground

So say my name
And every colour illuminates
And we are shining
And we'll never be afraid again
Say my name
As every colour illuminates

Say my name
As every colour illuminates
We are shining
And we will never be afraid again

Say my name
As every colour illuminates
We are shining
And we will never be afraid again

Say my name
We are shining
Say my name
Say my name

And we will never be afraid again

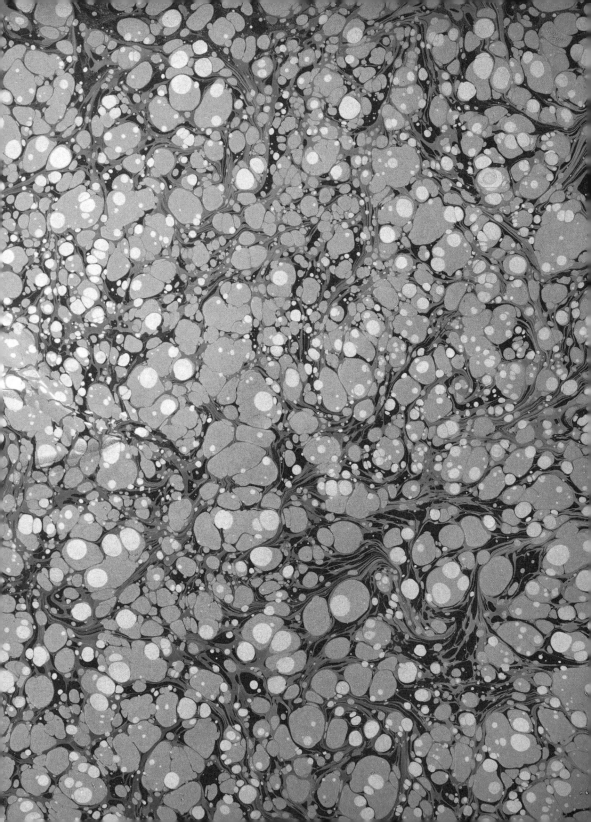

ALL THIS AND HEAVEN TOO

And the heart is hard to translate
It has a language of its own
It talks in tongues and quiet sighs
And prayers and proclamations, in the grand deeds
Of great men and the smallest of gestures
In short shallow gasps

But with all my education
I can't seem to commend it
And the words are all escaping me
And coming back all damaged
And I would put them back in poetry
If I only knew how, I can't seem to understand it

And I would give all this and heaven too
I would give it all if only for a moment
That I could just understand
The meaning of the word you see
'Cause I've been scrawling it forever
But it never makes sense to me at all

And it talks to me in tiptoes
And sings to me inside
It cries out in the darkest night
And breaks in the morning light

But with all my education
I can't seem to commend it
And the words are all escaping

And coming back all damaged
And I would put them back in poetry
If I only knew how, I can't seem to understand it

And I would give all this and heaven too
I would give it all if only for a moment
That I could just understand
The meaning of the word you see
'Cause I've been scrawling it forever
But it never makes sense to me at all

And I would give all this and heaven too
I would give it all if only for a moment
That I could just understand
The meaning of the word you see
'Cause I've been scrawling it forever
But it never makes sense to me at all

Oh, poor language
It doesn't deserve such treatment
And all my stumbling phrases
Never amounted to anything worth this feeling
Oh words were never so useful
So I was screaming out a language
That I never knew existed before

ONE
GRAND
MOMENT
IS
ALL I ASK

LEAVE MY BODY

I'm gonna be released from behind these eyes
And don't care whether I live or die
And I'm losing blood, I'm gonna leave my bones
And I don't want your heart, it leaves me cold

I don't want your future
I don't need your past
One grand moment is all I ask

I'm gonna leave my body (Moving up to higher ground)
I'm gonna lose my mind (History keeps pulling me down)
Said I'm gonna leave my body (Moving up to higher ground)
I'm gonna lose my mind (History keeps pulling me, pulling me down)

I don't need a husband, don't need no wife
And I don't need the day, I don't need the night
And I don't need the birds, let them fly away
And I don't want the clouds, they never seem to stay

I don't want no future (Want your future)
I don't need no past (Need no past)
(One grand moment) is all I ask
I don't want no future (Want your future)
I don't need no past (Need no past)
(One grand moment) is all I ask

I'm gonna leave my body (Moving up to higher ground)
I'm gonna lose my mind (History keeps pulling me down)
Said I'm gonna leave my body (Moving up to higher ground)
I'm gonna lose my, lose my mind (History keeps pulling me, pulling me down)

Pulling me down (And it's pulling me down)
Pulling me down (And it's pulling me down)
Pulling me down (And it's pulling me down)
Pulling me down, pulling me, pulling me down

I'm gonna leave my body (Moving up to higher ground)
I'm gonna lose my mind (History keeps pulling me down)
Said I'm gonna leave my body (Moving up to higher ground)
I'm gonna lose my mind (History keeps pulling me, pulling me down)

Said I'm gonna leave my body (Moving up to higher ground)
Gonna lose my mind (History keeps pulling me down)
Moving up to higher ground, history keeps pulling me, pulling me down

HOW BIG HOW BLUE HOW BEAUTIFUL

SHIP TO WRECK

Don't touch the sleeping pills
They mess with my head
Dredging up great white sharks
Swimming in the bed

Here comes a killer whale
To sing me to sleep
Thrashing the covers off
Has me by its teeth

And oh
My love remind me
What was it that I said
I can't help but pull the earth around me
To make my bed

And oh my love remind me
What was it that I did
I can't help but pull the earth around me
To make my bed

And oh my love remind me
What was it that I said
Did I drink too much
Am I losing touch
Did I build a ship to wreck

What's with the long face
Do you want more
Thousands of red-eyed mice
Scratching at the door

Don't let the curtain catch you
'Cause you've been here before
The chair is an island, darling
You can't touch the floor

And oh my love remind me
What was it that I did
I can't help but pull the earth around me
To make my bed

And oh my love remind me
What was it that I said
Did I drink too much
Am I losing touch
Did I build a ship to wreck

And good God
Under starless sky we are lost
And into the breach we got tossed
And the waters coming in fast

And oh my love remind me
What was it that I did
I can't help but pull the earth around me
To make my bed

And oh my love remind me
What was it that I said
Did I drink too much
Am I losing touch
Did I build a ship to wreck

I feel all at sea

I'm going to cross

a few to feel

better . . .

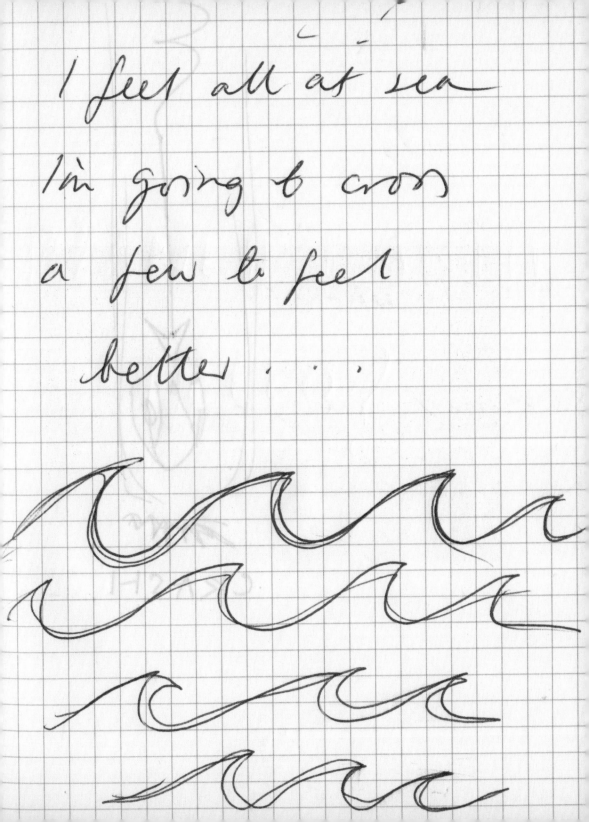

Chateau
Marmont
Hotel

Chateau Marmont

8221 Sunset Boulevard Hollywood California 90046
Telephone (323) 656-1010 Facsimile (323) 655-5311

In Residence
Mr. ~~Ross Levine~~
HAYCOCK

WHAT KIND OF MAN

LOVES LIKE THIS

WHAT KIND OF MAN

I was on a heavy tip
Trying to cross the canyon with a broken limb
You were on the other side like always
Wondering what to do with life
I'd already had a sip
So I reasoned I was drunk enough to deal with it
You were on the other side like always
You could never make your mind

And with one kiss
You inspired a fire of devotion
That lasts for twenty years
What kind of man loves like this

To let me dangle
At a cruel angle
My feet don't touch the floor
Sometimes you're half in
And then you're half out
But you never close the door

What kind of man loves like this
What kind of man
What kind of man loves like this
What kind of man

You holy fool
All coloured blue
Red feet upon the floor
You do such damage
How do you manage
To have me crawling back for more

And with one kiss
You inspired a fire of devotion
That lasts for twenty years
What kind of man loves like this

What kind of man loves like this
What kind of man
What kind of man loves like this
What kind of man

But I can't beat ya
'Cause I'm still with ya
Oh mercy, I implore
How do you do it
I think I'm through it
Then I'm back back back against the wall

What kind of man loves like this
What kind of man
What kind of man loves like this
What kind of man

What kind of man loves like this
What kind of man
What kind of man loves like this
What kind of man

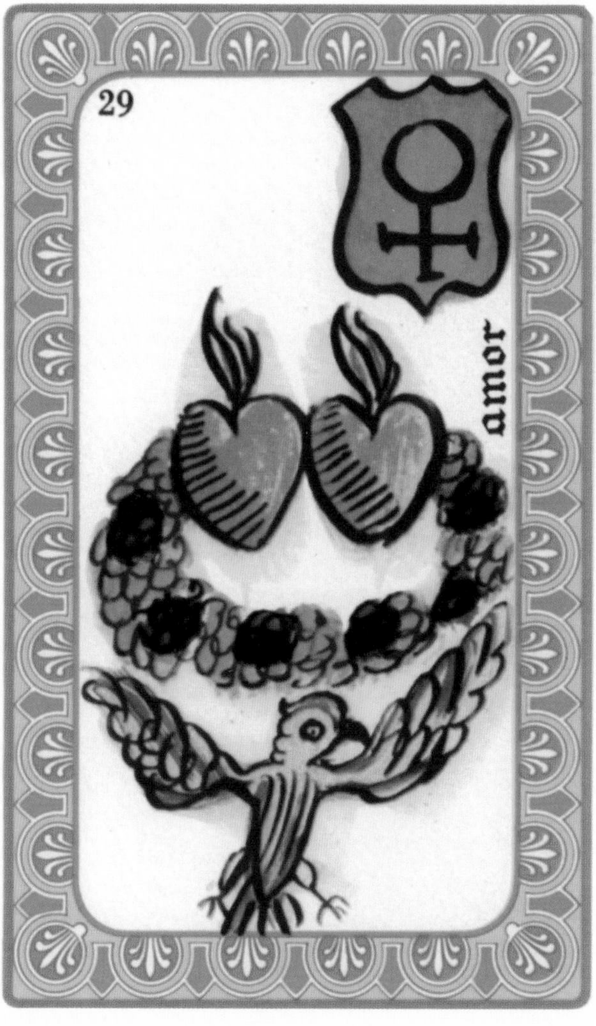
29
amor

OH
WHAT
IT IS
TO LOVE LIKE
THIS
REACHING
OUT MY ARMS
OH YOU
DEVASTATE

A CRUSEFIX AND
THE HOLLYWOOD
SIGN.

at least we'll always
have that
between us.

HOLLYWOOD

HOW BIG HOW BLUE HOW BEAUTIFUL

Between a crucifix and the Hollywood sign
We decided to get hurt
Now there's a few things we have to burn
Set our hearts ablaze

And every city was a gift
And every skyline was like a kiss upon the lips
And I was making you a wish
In every skyline

And meanwhile a man was falling from space
And every day I wore your face
Like an atmosphere around me
A satellite beside me
And meanwhile a man was falling from space
As he hit the earth I left this place
Let the atmosphere surround me
A satellite beside me

What are we gonna do?
We've opened the door and now it's all coming through
Tell me you see it too
We've opened our eyes and it's changing the view

How big
How blue
How beautiful

And meanwhile a man was falling from space
And every day I wore your face
Like an atmosphere around me
A satellite beside me
And meanwhile a man was falling from space
As he hit the earth I left this place
Let the atmosphere surround me
A satellite beside me

What are we gonna do?
We've opened the door and now it's all coming through
Tell me you see it too
We've opened our eyes and it's changing the view

How big
How blue
How beautiful

So much time on the other side
Waiting for you to wake up
So much time on the other side

Maybe I'll see you in another life
If this one wasn't enough
So much time on the other side

How big
How blue
How beautiful

HOW BIG
HOW BLUE
HOW BEAUTIFUL
HOW BEAUTIFUL

Datum / Date:

pure feeling

Chateau Marmont
8221 Sunset Boulevard   Hollywood California 90046
Telephone (323) 656-1010   Facsimile (323) 655-5311

In Residence :
Ms. Florence Welch

To give yourself over to another
Body
That's all you want really,
To be out of your own and
consumed by another..
To swim inside the skin of your lover...
Not have to break
Not have to think..
But you can't live on love
and salt water's no drink.
We're dying of thirst so we
feast on each other,
the sea is still our violent mother
The blood ruined here pours down
like water, each wave a lamb
led to the slaughter...
and like children that she just
can't teach....
We break, and break, and break
and break ourselves upon the beach....

F. Wx

QUEEN OF PEACE

Oh the king, gone mad within his suffering
Called out for release
Someone cure him of his grief
His only son, cut down but the battle won
Oh what is it worth
When all that's left is hurt

Like the stars chase the sun
Over the glowing hill I will conquer
Blood is running deep
Some things never sleep

Suddenly I'm overcome
Dissolving like the setting sun
Like a boat into oblivion
'Cause you're driving me away

Now you have me on the run
The damage is already done
Come on is this what you want
'Cause you're driving me away

Oh the queen of peace
Always does her best to please
It isn't any use
Somebody's gotta lose
Like a long scream
Out there always echoing
Oh what is it worth
When all that's left is hurt

Like the stars chase the sun
Over the glowing hill I will conquer
Love is running deep
Some things never sleep

Suddenly I'm overcome
Dissolving like the setting sun
Like a boat into oblivion
'Cause you're driving me away

Now you have me on the run
The damage is already done
Come on is this what you want
'Cause you're driving me away

And my love is no good
Against the fortress that it made of you
Blood is running deep
The sorrow that you keep

Suddenly I'm overcome
Dissolving like the setting sun
Like a boat into oblivion
'Cause you're driving me away

Now you have me on the run
The damage is already done
Come on is this what you want
'Cause you're driving me away

VARIOUS STORMS & SAINTS

And the air was full of various storms and saints
Parading in the street
As the banks begin to break
And I'm in the throes of it
Somewhere in the belly of the beast

But you took your toll on me
So I gave myself over willingly
You got a hold on me
I don't know how I don't just stand outside and scream
I am teaching myself how to be free

The monument of the memory
You tear it down in your head
Don't make the mountain your enemy
Get out, get up there instead

You saw the stars out in front of you
Too tempting not to touch
But even though it shocked you
Something's electric in your blood

Can people just untie themselves
Uncurling like flowers
If you could just forgive yourself

But still you stumble, your feet give way
Outside the world seems a violent place
You had to have him and so you did
Some things you let go in order to live

While all around you the buildings sway
Singing out loud, who made us this way?
I know you're bleeding but you'll be OK
Hold on to your heart, you'll keep it safe
Hold on to your heart, don't give it away

Now find a rooftop to sing from
Now find a hallway to dance
You don't need no edge to cling from
Your heart is there, it's in your hands

I know it seems like forever
I know it seems like an age
But one day this will be over
I swear it's not so far away

Can people just untie themselves
Uncurling like flowers
If you could just forgive yourself

And so you stumble, your feet give way
Outside the world seems a violent place
You had to have him and so you did
Some things you let go in order to live

While all around you the buildings sway
Singing out loud, who made us this way?
I know you're bleeding but you'll be OK
Hold on to your heart, you'll keep it safe
Hold on to your heart

DELILAH

Drifting through the hall with the sunrise
Holding on for your call
Climbing up the walls for that flashing light
I can never let go

'Cause I'm gonna be free and I'm gonna be fine
But maybe not tonight

It's a different kind of danger
And the bells are ringing out
And I'm calling for my mother
As I pull the pillars down

It's a different kind of danger
And my feet are spinning round
Never knew I was a dancer
Till Delilah showed me how

Too fast for freedom
Sometimes it all falls down
These chains never leave me
I keep dragging them around

Now it's one more boy and it's one more line
Taking the pills just to pass the time
I can never say no
'Cause I'm gonna be free and I'm gonna be fine
But maybe not tonight

Now I'm dancing with Delilah and her vision is mine
Holding on for your call
A different kind of danger in the daylight
I can never let go
Take anything to cut you I can find
Holding on for your call
A different kind of danger in the daylight

I'm strung up, strung out for your love
Hanging, hung up
It's so rough
I'm wrung and wringing out
Why can't you let me know
Strung up, strung out for your love
Hanging, hung up
It's so rough
Why can't you let me know

It's a different kind of danger
And the bells are ringing out
And I'm calling for my mother
As I pull the pillars down

It's a different kind of danger
And my feet are spinning round
Never knew I was a dancer
Till Delilah showed me how

Too fast for freedom
Sometimes it all falls down
These chains never leave me
I keep dragging them around

TOO
FAST
FOR
FREEDOM.

Delilah

ONE MORE
LIE
Hollywood
TOLD ME
ONE MORE G-D LIE

LONG AND LOST

Lost in the fog, these hollow hills
Blood running hot, night chills
Without your love I'll be
So long and lost, are you missing me

It's too late to come on home
All those bridges now old stones
It's too late to come on home
Can the city forgive,
I hear its sad song

I need the clouds to cover me
Pulling them down, surround me
Without your love I'll be
So long and lost, are you missing me

It's too late to come on home
All those bridges now old stones
It's too late to come on home
Can the city forgive, I hear its sad song

It's been so long between the words we spoke
Will you be there upon the shore, I hope
You wonder why it is that I came home
I figured out where I belonged

And it's too late to come on home
All those bridges now old stones
But it's too late to come on home
Can the city forgive, I hear its sad song

DREAD
BLUE
SKY'S

CAUGHT

It's the hardest thing I ever had to do
To try and keep from calling you
Well, can my dreams keep coming true
How can they, 'cause when I sleep
I never dream of you

As if the dream of you, it sleeps too
But it never slips away
It just gains its strength and digs its hooks
To drag me through the day

And I'm caught
I forget all that I've been taught
I can't keep calm, I can't keep still
Pulled apart against my will

It's the hardest thing I've ever had to prove
You turned to salt as I turned round to look at you
Old friends have said the books I've read
Say it's the thing to do
But it's hard to see it when you're in it
'Cause I went blind for you

Then you leave my head and crawl out the bed
You subconscious solipsist
And for those hours deep in the dark
Perhaps you don't exist

But I'm caught
I forget all that I've been taught
I can't keep calm, I can't keep still
Pulled apart against my will

And I'm thrashing on the line
Somewhere between desperate and divine
I can't keep calm, I can't keep still
Persephone will have her fill

And I'm caught
I forget all that I've been taught
I can't keep calm, I can't keep still
Pulled apart against my will

And I'm caught
I forget all that I've been taught
I can't keep calm, I can't keep still
Pulled apart against my will

ZAP

Datum / Date:

You saw a star
at in front yr
~~to of~~ ~~to empting~~ ~~to~~
so tempting ~~not forbidden~~
~~too~~
an even though it
~~all your~~ ~~over your~~
~~shok~~ shocked
~~it was worth it~~ you
~~it was~~
~~you didn't~~
~~spill too much~~

~~Some things are~~
~~worth~~
~~a little blood~~

THIRD EYE

That original lifeline
Original lifeline
That original lifeline

Hey look up, don't make a shadow of yourself
Always shutting out the light
Caught in your own creation
Look up, look up, it tore you open

And oh how much
'Cause there's a hole where your heart lies
And I can see it with my third eye
And oh my touch, it magnifies
You pull away, you don't know why

That original lifeline
Original lifeline
That original lifeline

Hey look up, you don't have to be a ghost
Here amongst the living
You are flesh and blood
And you deserved to be loved
And you deserve what you are given

And oh how much
'Cause there's a hole where your heart lies
And I can see it with my third eye
And oh my touch, it magnifies
You pull away, you don't know why

That original lifeline
Original lifeline
That original lifeline
Original lifeline

'Cause there's a hole where your heart lies
And I can see it with my third eye
And oh my touch, it magnifies
You pull away, you don't know why

That original lifeline
Original lifeline
That original lifeline
Original lifeline

Because your pain is a tribute
The only thing you let hold you
Wear it now like a mantle
Always there to remind you

That your pain is a tribute
The only thing you let hold you
Wear it now like a mantle
Always there to remind you

I am the same, I'm the same
I'm trying to change
I am the same, I'm the same
I'm trying to change
I am the same, I'm the same
I'm trying to change
I am the same, I'm the same
I'm trying to change

'Cause there's a hole where your heart lies
And I can see it with my third eye
And oh my touch, it magnifies
You pull away, you don't know why

I am the same, I'm the same
I'm trying to change

AND OH

HOW

MUCH

HOLLYWOOD
SPECIAL GUEST

151

HELL
Grand Cayman B.W.I.

ISN'T IT

A DREAM TO BE

ALIVE

ST JUDE

Another conversation with no destination
Another battle never won
Each side is a loser
So who cares who fired the gun?

And I'm learning so I'm leaving
And even though I'm grieving
I'm trying to find the meaning
Letting loss reveal it
Letting loss reveal it

St Jude
The patron saint of the lost causes
St Jude
We were lost before she started
St Jude
We lay in bed as she whipped around us
St Jude
Maybe I've always been more comfortable in chaos

And I was on the island
And you were there too
But somehow through the storm
I couldn't get to you
St Jude
Somehow she knew

And she came to give her blessing
While causing devastation
And I couldn't keep my mouth shut
I just had to mention
Grabbing your attention

St Jude
The patron saint of the lost causes
St Jude
We were lost before she started
St Jude
We lay in bed as she whipped around us
St Jude
Maybe I've always been more comfortable in chaos

St Jude
St Jude
St Jude

And I'm learning so I'm leaving
And even though I'm grieving
I'm trying to find the meaning
Letting loss reveal it

And I'm learning so I'm leaving
And even though I'm grieving
I'm trying to find the meaning
Letting loss reveal it

MOTHER

Oh lord, won't you leave me
Leave me on my knees
'Cause I belong to the ground now
And it belongs to me

Oh lord, won't you leave me
Leave me just like this
'Cause I belong to the ground now
I want no more than this

And how long for the autumn
The sun keeps burning me
Every stone in this city
Keeps reminding me, oh

Can you protect me
From what I want
A lover I let in
Who left me so lost

Mother, make me
Make me a big tall tree
So I can shed my leaves
And let it blow through me

Mother, make me
Make me a big great cloud
So I can rain on you
Things I can't say out loud

All these couples are kissing
And I can't stand the heat
I lost my shoes and left the party
I wandered in the street

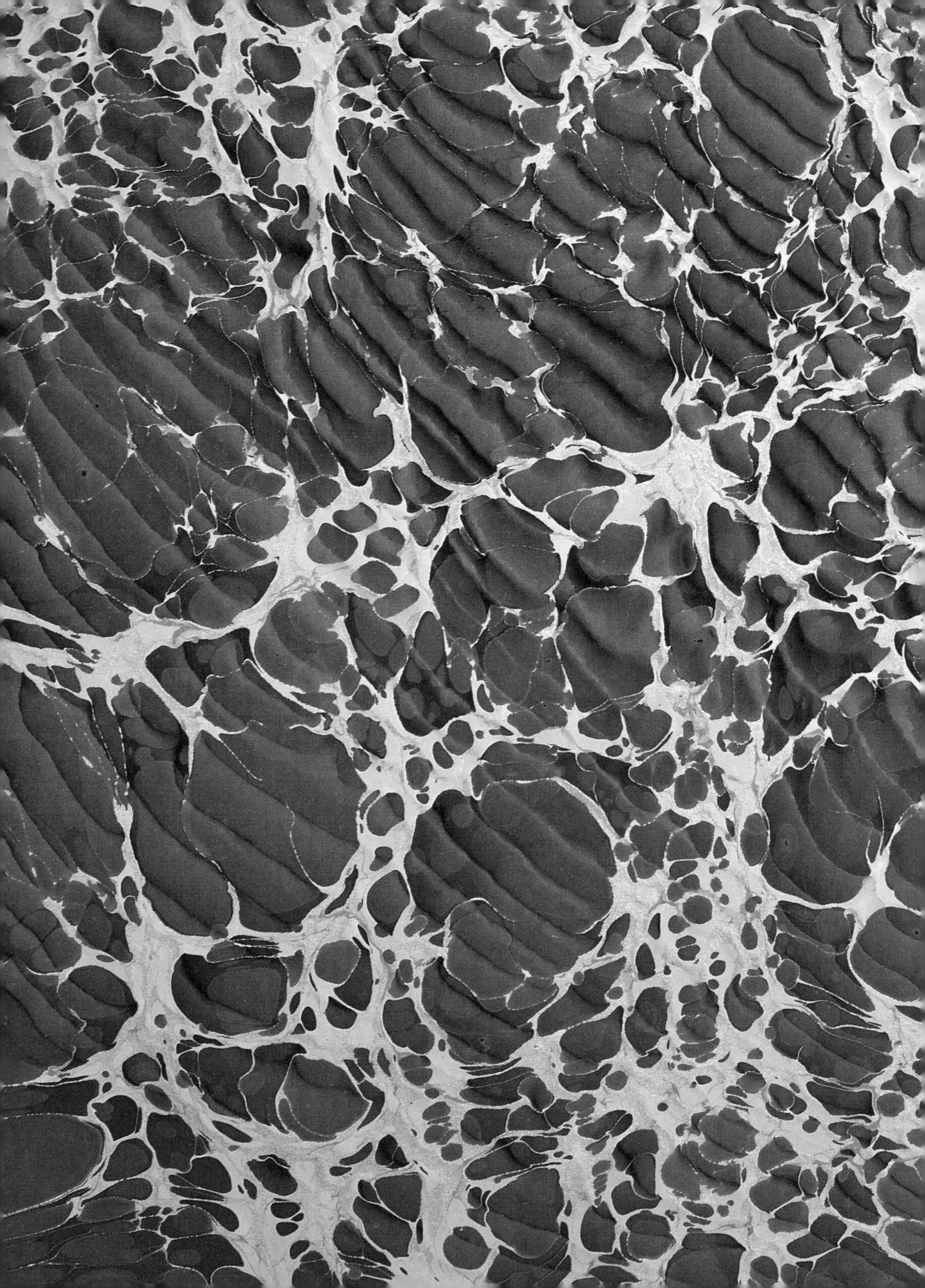

I put my feet into the fountain
The statues all asleep
No use wishing on the water
Won't bring you no release

Mother, make me
Make me a bird of prey
So I can rise above this
Let it fall away

Mother, make me
Make me a song so sweet
Heaven trembles
Falling at my feet

Oh lord, won't you leave me
Leave me on my knees
'Cause I belong to the ground now
And it belongs to me

Oh lord, won't you leave me
Leave me just like this
'Cause I belong to the ground now
I want no more than this

Oh lord, won't you leave me
Leave me on my knees
'Cause I belong to the ground now
And it belongs to me

Oh lord, won't you leave me
Leave me just like this
'Cause I belong to the ground now
I want no more than this

Foxy
X

~~the pite~~

We cherished you Cake
when you got so tough

HEART HURTY

cracked egg heart

Who's

a heretic

NOW.

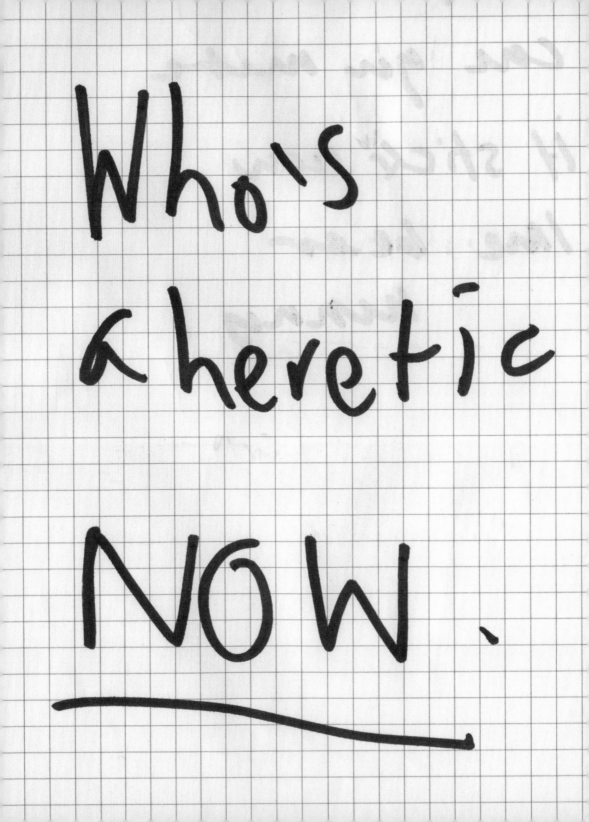

Witchcraft

. . . . . .

you put a
girdle ~~around~~ about
the earth in
forty minutes . . .
midsummer nights dream . .

WHICH WITCH

And it's my whole heart
Weighed and measured inside
And it's an old scar
Trying to bleach it out
And it's my whole heart
Deemed and delivered a crime
I'm on trial, waiting till the beat comes out
I'm on trial, waiting till the beat comes out

Who's a heretic now
Am I making sense
How can you make it stick
Waiting till the beat comes out
Who's a heretic, child?
Can you make it stick, now
And I'm on trial
Waiting till the beat comes out

I'm miles away, he's on my mind
I'm getting tired of crawling all the way
And I've had enough, it's obvious
And I'm getting tired of crawling all the way
Crawling all the way
Crawling all the way

I'm miles away, he's on my mind
I'm getting tired of crawling all the way
And I've had enough, it's obvious
And I'm getting tired of crawling all the way
Crawling all the way
Crawling all the way

I'm not beaten by this yet
You can't tell me to regret
Been in the dock since the day we met
Fire, help me to forget

I'm not beaten by this yet
You can't tell me to regret
Been in the dock since the day we met
Fire, help me to forget

And it's my whole heart
While tried and tested, it's mine
And it's my whole heart
Trying to reach it out
And it's my whole heart
Burned but not buried this time
I'm on trial, waiting till the beat comes out
I'm on trial, waiting till the beat comes out

I'm miles away, he's on my mind
I'm getting tired of crawling all the way
And I've had enough, it's obvious
And I'm getting tired of crawling all the way
Crawling all the way
Crawling all the way

I'm not beaten by this yet
You can't tell me to regret
Been in the dock since the day we met
Fire, help me to forget

I'm not beaten by this yet
You can't tell me to regret
Been in the dock since the day we met
Fire, help me to forget

Chained and shackled, oh
I'll unravel, oh
It's a pity, oh
Never to return
But I never learn
It's a pity, oh

Chained and shackled, oh
I'll unravel, oh
It's a pity, oh
Say I won't return
But I never learn
It's a pity, oh

Passi
agres
cares

the
tea . . . x

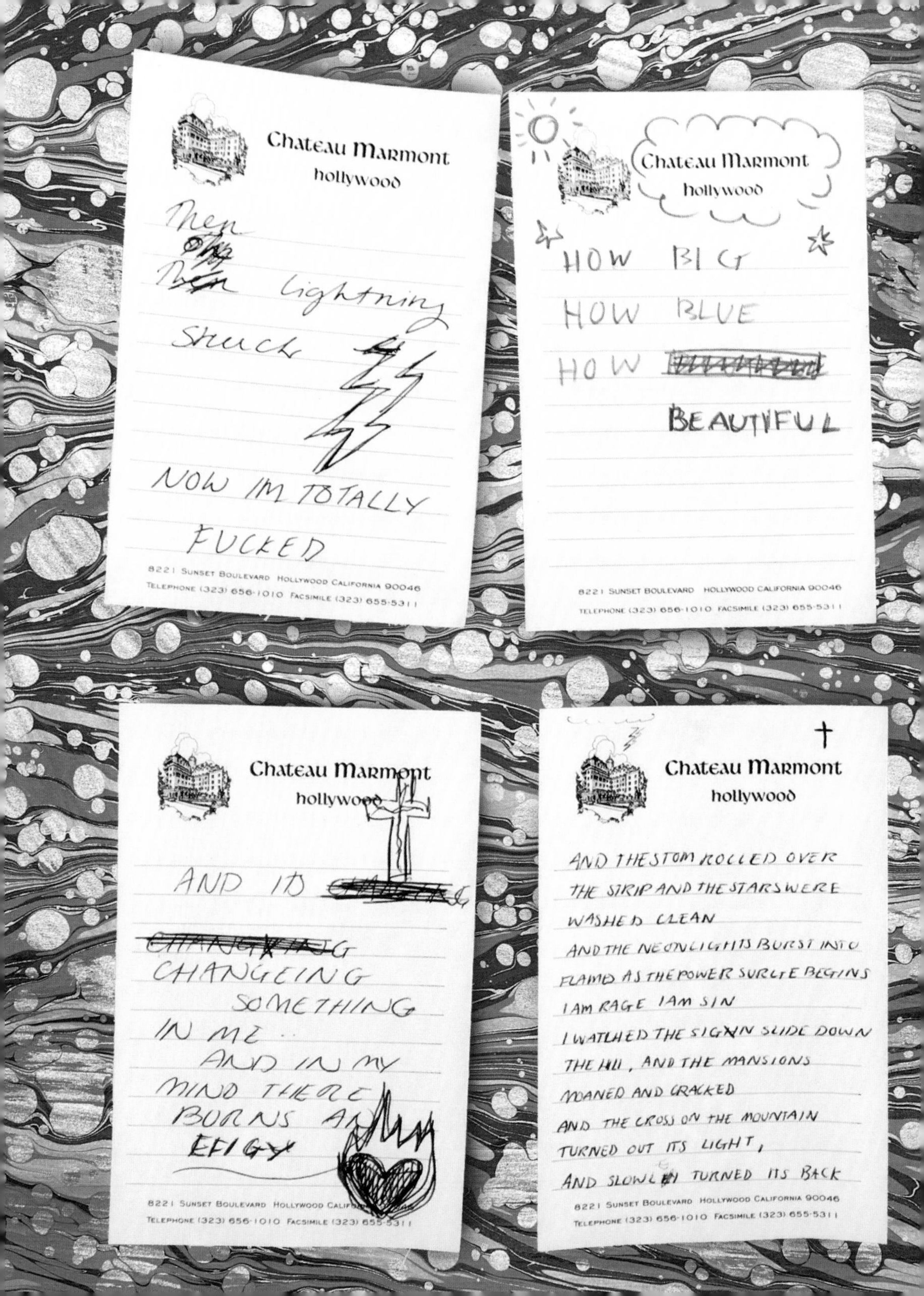
Chateau Marmont
hollywood
Men
lightning
struck
NOW IM TOTALLY
FUCKED
8221 Sunset Boulevard Hollywood California 90046
Telephone (323) 656-1010 Facsimile (323) 655-5311
Chateau Marmont
hollywood
HOW BIG
HOW BLUE
HOW
BEAUTIFUL
8221 Sunset Boulevard Hollywood California 90046
Telephone (323) 656-1010 Facsimile (323) 655-5311
Chateau Marmont
hollywood
AND ITS
CHANGEING
SOMETHING
IN ME..
AND IN MY
MIND THERE
BURNS AN
EFIGY
8221 Sunset Boulevard Hollywood California
Telephone (323) 656-1010 Facsimile (323) 655-5311
Chateau Marmont
hollywood
AND THE STOM ROLLED OVER
THE STRIP AND THE STARS WERE
WASHED CLEAN
AND THE NEON LIGHTS BURST INTO
FLAME AS THE POWER SURGE BEGINS
I AM RAGE I AM SIN
I WATCHED THE SIGN SLIDE DOWN
THE HILL, AND THE MANSIONS
MOANED AND CRACKED
AND THE CROSS ON THE MOUNTAIN
TURNED OUT ITS LIGHT,
AND SLOWLY TURNED ITS BACK
8221 Sunset Boulevard Hollywood California 90046
Telephone (323) 656-1010 Facsimile (323) 655-5311

Chateau Marmont
hollywood
eye's so full of
Sunrise
couldn't shed
a single tear
8221 Sunset Boulevard Hollywood California 90046
Telephone (323) 656-1010 Facsimile (323) 655-5311
Chateau Marmont
hollywood
CHAOS
MAGIC
8221 Sunset Boulevard Hollywood California 90046
Telephone (323) 656-1010 Facsimile (323) 655-5311
Chateau Marmont
hollywood
THE END
OF
LOVE
8221 Sunset Boulevard Hollywood California 90046
Telephone (323) 656-1010 Facsimile (323) 655-5311
Chateau Marmont
hollywood
I let him
sleep and
My held breath
fills the room
with love...
8221 Sunset Boulevard Hollywood California 90046
Telephone (323) 656-1010 Facsimile (323) 655-5311

THERE CAN BE
NO LOVE IN
NEW YORK CITY
I DON'T SLEEP
I CHASE
The Bowery Hotel
335 THE BOWERY, NEW YORK CITY 10003
TEL: 212.505.9100 • FAX: 212.505.9700
THEBOWERYHOTEL.COM

HIGH AS HOPE

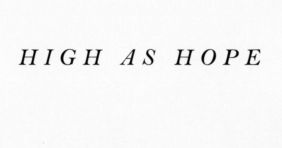

100 YEARS

I believe in you and in our hearts we know the truth
and I believe in love and the darker it gets the more I do
Try and fill us with your hate and we will shine a light
and the days will become endless, and never and never turn to night
and never, and never turn to night

Then it's just too much
I cannot get you close enough
100 arms
100 years
You can always find me here
Lord, don't let it break this
lemme hold it lightly
give me arms to pray with instead of ones that hold too tightly

We have no need to fight
We raise our voices and let our hearts take flight
Get higher than those planes can fly
where the stars do not take sides

Then it's just too much
I cannot get you close enough
100 arms
100 years
You can always find me here
And lord, don't let me break this
lemme hold it lightly
give me arms to pray with instead of ones that hold too tightly

And then it's just too much
The streets they still run with blood
100 arms
100 years
You can always find me here
And lord, don't let me break this
lemme hold it lightly
give me arms to pray with instead of ones that hold too tightly

I let him sleep and as he does
My held breath fills the room with love
It hurts in ways I can't describe
My heart bends and breaks
So many many times
And is born again with each sunrise
Funerals were held all over the city
The youth bleeding in the square
and women raged as old men fumbled and cried
we're sorry we thought you didn't care
And how does it feel now you've scratched that itch
and pulled out all your stitches
Hubris is a bitch

100 arms
100 years
100 arms
100 years

And then it's just too much, the streets they still run with blood
100 arms
100 years
You can always find me here
And lord, don't let me break this
lemme hold it lightly
give me arms to pray with instead of ones that hold too tightly

ALWAYS
LONELY

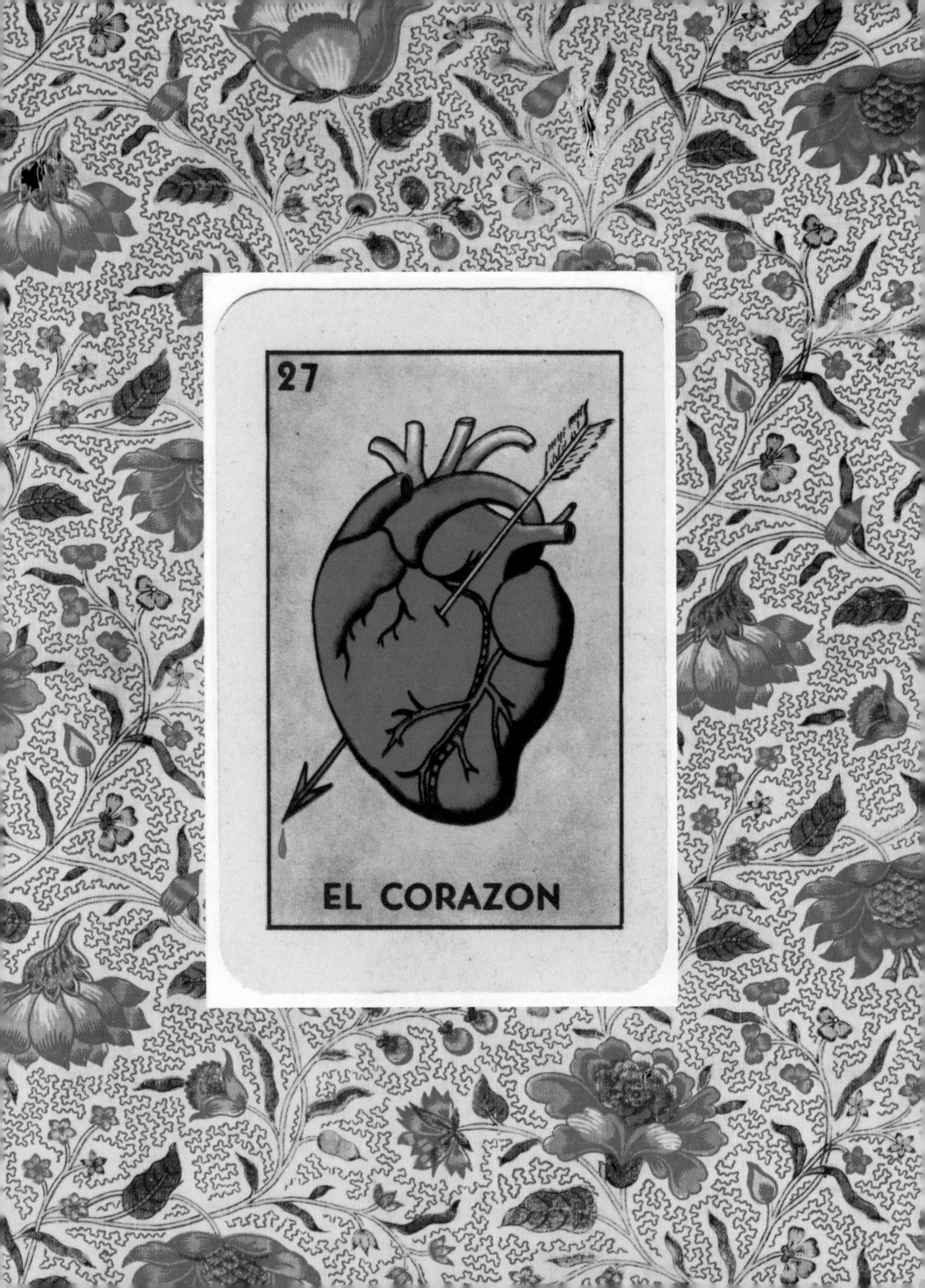
27
EL CORAZON

BIG GOD

You need a big God
big enough to hold your love
You need a big God
big enough to fill you up

You keep me up at night, to my messages you do not reply
You know I still like you the most
the best of the best and the worst of the worst

You can never know the places that I go
I still like you the most
You'll always be my favourite ghost

You need a big God
big enough to hold your love
You need a big God
big enough to fill you up

Sometimes I think it's getting better and then it gets much worse
Is it just part of the process?
Jesus Christ it hurts
though I know I should know better
Well, I can make this work
Is it just part of the process?

Jesus Christ, Jesus Christ it hurts
Jesus Christ, Jesus Christ it hurts

You need a big God
big enough to hold your love
You need a big God
big enough to fill you up

Shower your affection, let it rain on me
Pull down the mountain, drag your cities to the sea

Shower your affection, let it rain on me
Don't leave me on this white cliff
Let it slide down to the, slide down to the sea
slide down to the, slide down to the sea

SHADES OF ETERNAL NIGHT

I feel the
clouds collecting
let it rain
on me.

and wash away
the mountains
~~and the~~ let them
~~cities to~~ the slide
~~sea~~ : down
to the
sea.

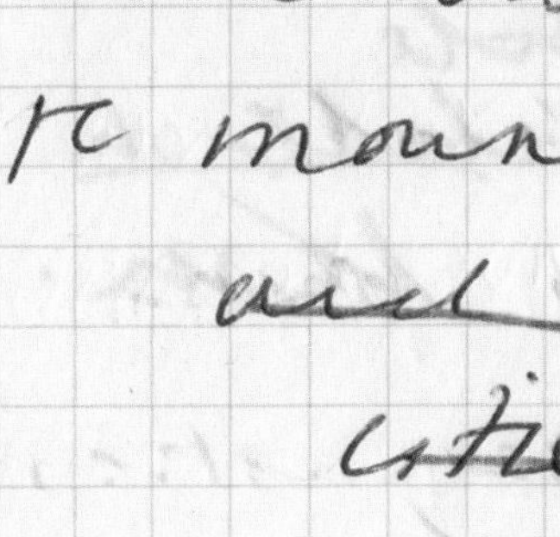

I feel the clouds
collecting
let it rain on me

I HAVE
ONLY
EVER TRIED
TO SHOW
YOU
BEAUTY

SNAKES

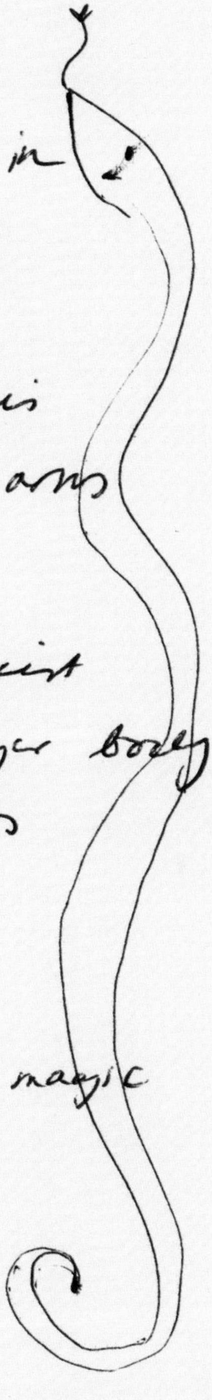

and it begins,
I start to breath it in
twisting like snakes

and what it is
a creature like this
a hundred grasping arms
oh they devastate

where does the anger exist
in the movement of your body
in the swinging of your hips
its at my fingertips
then its on my lips

what reckless restless magic
is this ....

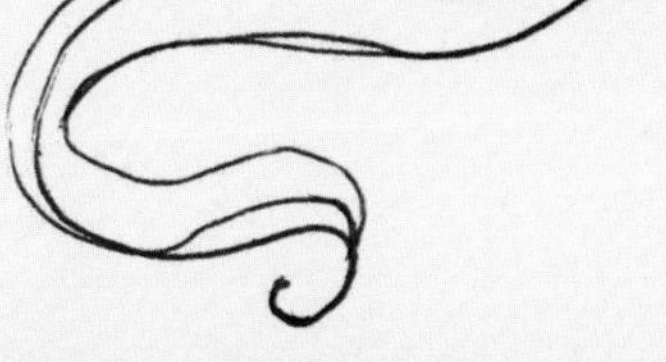

GRACE

I'm sorry I ruined your birthday
I guess I could go back to university
try and make my mother proud
stop this phase I'm in she deems dangerous and loud

The spelling is a problem
as is the discipline
I don't think it would be too long
before I was drunk in Camberwell again

This is the only thing I've ever had any faith in
Grace, I know you carry us
Grace, and it was such a mess
Grace, I don't say it enough
Grace, you are so loved

I'm sorry I ruined your birthday, you had turned eighteen
and the sunshine hit me and I was behaving strangely
All the walls were melting and there were mermaids everywhere
Hearts flew from my hands, and I could see people's feelings

This is the only thing I've ever had any faith in
Grace, I know you carry us
Grace, and it was such a mess
Grace, I don't say it enough

Grace, you are so loved
And you, you were the one I treated the worst
only because you loved me the most
We haven't spoken in a long time
I think about it sometimes

I don't know who I was back then
and I hope and hope
I would never treat anyone like that again

This is the only thing I've ever had any faith in
Grace, I know you carry us
Grace, and it was such a mess
Grace, I don't say it enough
Grace, you are so loved

Grace, I know you carry us
Grace, and it was such a fucking mess
Grace, I don't say it enough
Grace, you are so loved

This is the only thing I've ever had any faith in
this is the only thing I've ever had any faith in
this is the only thing I've ever had any faith in
this is the only thing I've ever had any faith in

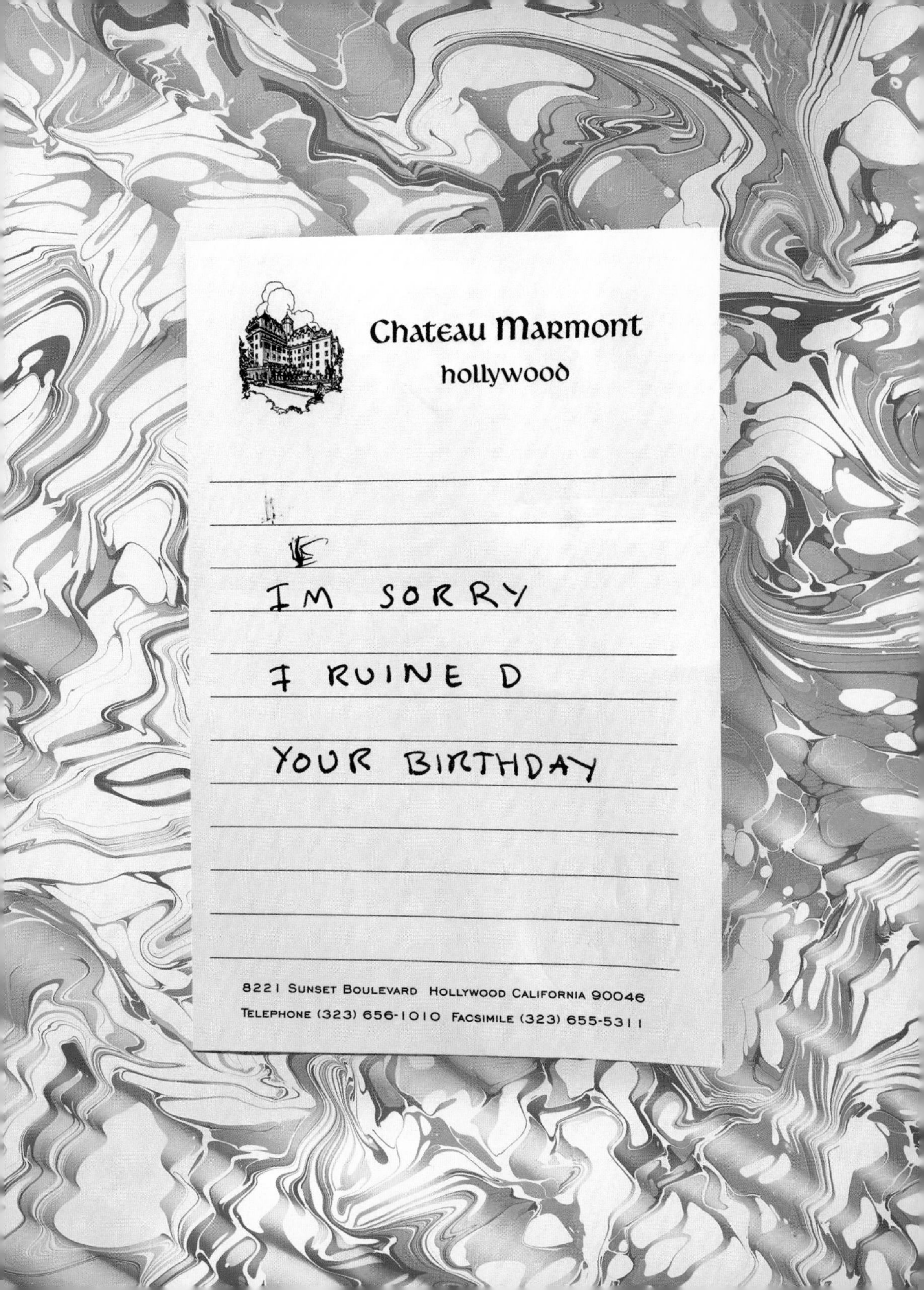
Chateau Marmont
hollywood

IM SORRY
I RUINE D
YOUR BIRTHDAY

8221 SUNSET BOULEVARD HOLLYWOOD CALIFORNIA 90046
TELEPHONE (323) 656-1010 FACSIMILE (323) 655-5311

HUNGER

At seventeen I started to starve myself
I thought that love was a kind of emptiness
At least I understood then the hunger I felt
and I didn't have to call it loneliness

We all have a hunger
we all have a hunger
we all have a hunger
we all have a hunger

Tell me what you need
Oh, you look so free
the way you use your body, baby
Come on and work it for me
Don't let them get you down
You're the best thing I've seen
We never found the answer
but we knew one thing

We all have a hunger
we all have a hunger
we all have a hunger
we all have a hunger

And it's Friday night and it's kicking in
In that pink dress they're gonna crucify me
Oh and you in all your vibrant youth

How could anything bad ever happen to you?
You make a fool of death with your beauty
And for a moment, I thought that love was in the drugs
but the more I took the more it took away and I could never get enough

I thought that love was on a stage, give yourself to strangers
You don't have to be afraid
then it tries to find a home
with people or when I'm alone
picking it apart
and staring at your phone

We all have a hunger
we all have a hunger
we all have a hunger
we all have a hunger

Tell me what you need
Oh, you look so free
the way you use your body, baby
Come on and work it for me

Don't let them get you down
You're the best thing I've seen
We never found the answer
But we knew one thing

We all have a hunger
we all have a hunger
we all have a hunger
we all have a hunger

And it's Friday night and it's kicking in
In that pink dress they're gonna crucify me
Oh and you in all your vibrant youth

How could anything bad ever happen to you?
You make a fool of death with your beauty
And for a moment I forget to worry

NO ONE IS COMING TO SAVE YOU
Virgin Mary of Camberwell

IM ALWAYS

DOWN TO

HIDE WITH

YOU.

YOUR SO HIGH

YOUR SO HIGH

YOUR SO HIGH

YOUR SO HIGH

SKYSCRAPERS
LOOK ON LIKE
GREAT UNBLINKING
GIANTS
IN THOSE HEAVY
DAYS IN JUNE.
WHEN LOVE
BECAME AN ACT
OF DEFIANCE.

JUNE

The show was ending and I had started to crack
Woke up in Chicago when the sky turned black
And you're so high, you're so high, you have to be an angel
And I'm so high, I'm so high, I can see an angel

I hear your heart beating in your chest
The world slows till there's nothing left
Skyscrapers look on like great unblinking giants
in those heavy days in June, when love became an act of defiance

Hold on to each other
hold on to each other
hold on to each other
hold on to each other

And you were broken-hearted
and the world was too
And I was beginning to lose my grip
and I have always held it loosely

But this time I admit
I felt it really start to slip
And choirs sing in the street
and I would come to you, to watch the television screen
in your hotel room
I'm always down to hide with you

Hold on to each other
hold on to each other
hold on to each other
hold on to each other

You're so high, you're so high
You're so high, you're so high
You're so high, you're so high
you have to be an angel

And I'm so high, I'm so high
I'm so high, I'm so high
I'm so high, I'm so high
I can see an angel

I SEE ANGELS
EVERYWHERE

THEY WALK THE
STREETS WITHOUT

~~THE~~ THEIR WINGS

I MET ONE CRYING
IN A HOTEL
BAR

TRYING TO EXPLAIN
THINGS

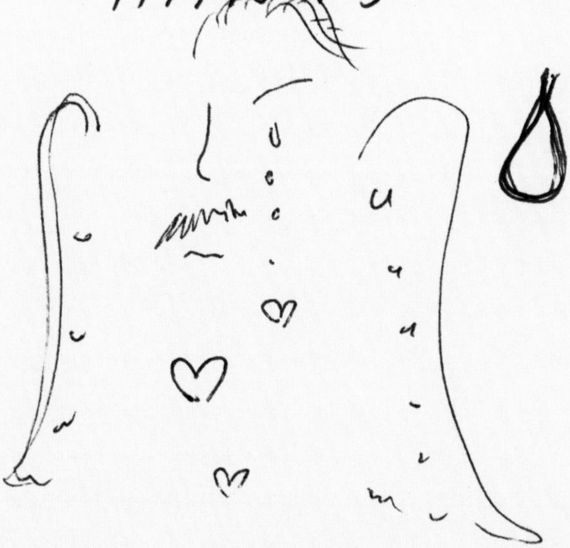

NO GOD'S

there is nothing I can do.
I was born to be your fool
because people like me
love people like you..

JESUS'S 

BLOOD

HAS NEVER

FAILED ME

YET

YMCA

PATRICIA

Oh Patricia, you've always been my North Star
and I have to tell you something: I'm still afraid of the dark
But you take my hand in your hand
from you the flowers grow
and do you understand with every seed you sow
you make this cold world
beautiful

You told me all doors are open to the believer
I believe her, I believe her, I believe her
You told me all doors are open to the believer
I believe her, I believe her, I believe her

Oh Patricia, you've always been my North Star
Oh Patricia, you've always been my North Star

Well, you're a real man and you do what you can
you only take as much as you can grab with two hands
With your big heart you praise God above
but how's that working out for you, honey
do you feel loved?

She told me all doors are open to the believer
I believe her, I believe her, I believe her
You told me our doors are open to the believer
I believe her, I believe her, I believe her

Oh Patricia, you've always been my North Star
Oh Patricia, you've always been my North Star

Drink too much coffee and think of you often
in a city where reality has long been forgotten
Are you afraid because I'm terrified?
You remind me that it's such a wonderful thing to love
it's such a wonderful thing to love
it's such a wonderful thing to love
it's such a wonderful thing to love
it's such a wonderful thing

9/10

FROM YOU
THE FLOWERS
GROW,
AND DO YOU
UNDESTAND
WITH EVERY
SEED YOU SOW
YOU MAKE THIS
COLD WORLD,
BEAUTIFUL.

Florence + the coffee machine

I could fall
in love
with a ~~paper~~ plastic
bag
if it paid
me some attention

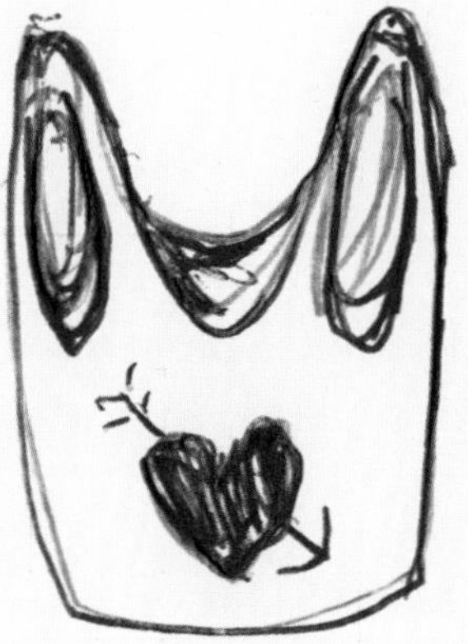

SKY FULL OF SONG

How deeply are you sleeping or are you still awake?
A good friend told me you've been staying out so late
Be careful oh my darling, oh be careful what it takes
from what I've seen so far the good ones always seem to break

And I was screaming at my father
and you were screaming at me
and I can feel your anger from way across the sea

And I was kissing strangers
I was causing such a scene
oh the heart, it hides such unimaginable things

Grab me by my ankles, I've been flying for too long
I couldn't hide from the thunder in a sky full of song
And I want you so badly but you could be anyone
I couldn't hide from the thunder in a sky full of song

Hold me down, I'm so tired now
Aim your arrow at the sky
Take me down, I'm too tired now
Leave me where I lie

And I can tell that I'm in trouble when that music starts to play
in a city without seasons, it keeps raining in LA
I feel like I'm about to fall, the room begins to sway
and I can hear the sirens but I cannot walk away

Grab me by my ankles, I've been flying for too long
I couldn't hide from the thunder in a sky full of song
And I want you so badly but you could be anyone
I couldn't hide from the thunder in a sky full of song

Hold me down, I'm so tired now
Aim your arrow at the sky
Take me down, I'm too tired now
Leave me where I lie

I thought I was flying but maybe I'm dying tonight
I thought I was flying but maybe I'm dying tonight
and I thought I was flying but maybe I'm dying tonight
I thought I was flying but maybe I'm dying tonight

Hold me down, I'm so tired now
Aim your arrow at the sky
Take me down, I'm too tired now
Leave me where I lie

Hold me down, I'm so tired now
Aim your arrow at the sky
Take me down, I'm too tired now
Leave me where I lie

The lazy
Buttered toast
smell of
someone you love . . .

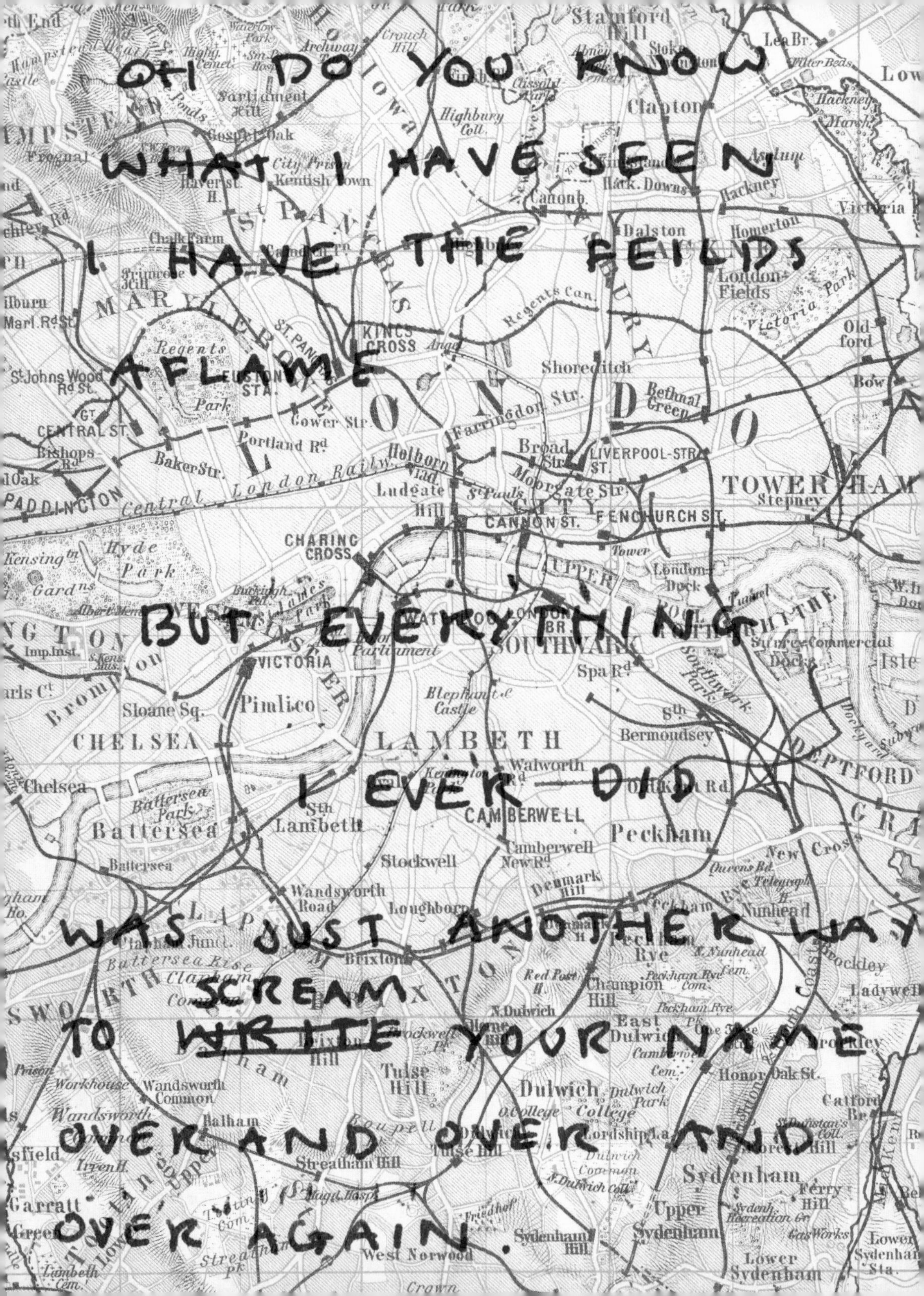
OH! DO YOU KNOW
WHAT I HAVE SEEN
I HAVE THE FEILDS
AFLAME
BUT EVERYTHING
I EVER DID
WAS JUST ANOTHER WAY
SCREAM
TO ~~WRITE~~ YOUR NAME
OVER AND OVER AND
OVER AGAIN.

SOUTH LONDON FOREVER

When I go home alone I drive past the place
where I was born
and the places that I used to drink
young and drunk and stumbling in the street
outside The Joiners Arms
like foals unsteady on their feet
With the art students and the boys in bands
high on E and holding hands with someone
that I just met
I thought it doesn't get better than this
there can be nothing better than this
better than this

We climbed onto the roof of the museum
and someone made love in the grass
and I forgot my name and the way back
to my mother's house
With your black pool eyes and your bitten lips
the world is at your fingertips
It doesn't get better than this
what else could be better than this

Oh do you know what I have seen
I have seen the fields aflame
and everything I ever did
was just another way to scream your name
over and over and over and over again
over and over and over and over again

And we're just children wanting children
of our own
I want a space to watch things grow
but did I dream too big, do I have to let it go
what if one day there is no such thing as snow
Oh God, what do I know

And I don't know anything
except that green is so green
and there's a special kind of sadness
that seems to come with spring

Oh do you know what I have seen
I have seen the fields aflame
and everything I ever did
was just another way to scream your name
over and over and over and over again
over and over and over and over again

Oh do you know what I have seen
I have seen the fields aflame
but everything I ever did
was just another way to scream your name

I DREAMT LAST
NIGHT OF A
BIG SIGN THAT
READ
'THE END OF LOVE'

I REMEMBER
THINKING
'THATS A GOOD
LYRIC I WISH I WROTE
THAT'

THE END OF LOVE

I feel nervous in a way that can't be named
I dreamt last night of a sign that read 'the end of love'
and I remember thinking, even in my dreaming
it was a good line for a song

We were a family pulled from the flood
You tore the floorboards up
and let the river rush in
not wash away, wash away

We were reaching in the dark
that summer in New York
and it was so far to fall
You said it didn't hurt at all
You let it wash away, wash away

In a moment of joy and fury
I threw myself on the balcony
like my grandmother some years before me
I've always been in love with you
Could you tell it from the moment that I met you?

We were a family pulled from the flood
you tore the floorboards up
and let the river rush in
not wash away, wash away

We were reaching in the dark
that summer in New York
and it was so far to fall
oh it didn't hurt at all
I let it wash away, wash away

And Joshua came down from the mountain
with a tablet in his hands
told me that he loved me
and then ghosted me again

We were reaching in the dark
that summer in New York
and it was so far to fall
You said it didn't hurt at all
I let it wash away, wash away

We were reaching in the dark
that summer in New York
and it was so far to fall
but it didn't hurt at all
I let it wash away, wash away

THE END
OF LOVE

NO CHOIR

And it's hard to write about being happy because the older I get
I find that happiness, is an extremely uneventful subject
and there would be no grand choirs to sing
no chorus could come in about two people, sitting doing nothing

But I must confess
I did it all for myself
I gathered you here
to hide from some vast unnameable fear

But the loneliness never left me
I always took it with me
but I can put it down in the pleasure of your company
and there will be no grand choirs to sing
no chorus will come in
no ballad will be written
it will be entirely forgotten
and if tomorrow it's all over
at least we had it for a moment
oh darling, things seem so unstable
but for a moment we were able to be still

And there will be no grand choirs to sing
no chorus will come in
no ballad will be written
this will be entirely forgotten

AND IF

TOMMOROW

ITS ALL OVER

AT LEAST WE HAD

IT FOR

A MOMENT

EVER
REACHING
HIGH AS
HOPE
The Bowery Hotel
335 THE BOWERY, NEW YORK CITY 10003
TEL: 212.505.9100 • FAX: 212.505.9700
THEBOWERYHOTEL.COM

POETRY

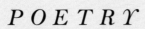

SONG CONTINUED

And this new voice
This 'me' voice
Is it conversational

Confessional?

Does it describe the Easter Sunday I had with Bryan Ferry,
Or that I slept in the corner of his studio once,
I was so hungover, I think he covered me with a scarf . . .

It also might have been Isaac,
But Bryan Ferry
is a good person
to put into a poem

What about the time I swam in the Cambridge river
with the students graduating . . .
Then left my stage clothes on the bus to Camberwell
In blackout,
After getting kicked out of Topshop for drinking rosé
in the changing rooms

The pair of knickers left somewhere in Peckham
after an aborted threesome.
The shoe that my ex-boyfriend
tried to hit my new boyfriend with,
On Valentine's Day,
outside my mum's house.

Various black eyes,
unexplainable love bites,
lost handbags/phones/cards/wraps
My college work abandoned so I didn't have to carry it home . . .

And other south London artefacts

I'm not sure I could put these things into a song . . .
These muddy trinkets
Not beautiful enough, too bloody and ragged . . .
I always felt the song should transcend the swamp.
I needed it to dredge me out.
Drain my lungs,
Massage my heart till I'd coughed it up.

Like
Ah.
Here it is.
Is it
enough

NEW YORK POEM (FOR POLLY)

My mother and father come to me in visions
and I can feel their arms of love stretch out across the sea,
across time, across divorces, deception and death.
And I know that I am their daughter.
And I know that they love me, despite the damage.

We walk past the hotel where we nearly died,
a kind of passive double suicide.
Wave at the ghosts of ourselves,
cold and still inside,
run screaming into the street,
THIS IS THE NEW SHIT.
Heady with pagan worship
of water towers,
fire escapes, ever reaching,
high as hope.

Then we are dead.
And we are together in 'other' New York.
Which is both heaven and hell,
and we have coffee and ice cream
and aching hearts.

MONARCH BUTTERFLIES

I am afraid of things being written down
Confined to the page so permanent
There is an impermanence to song
It is fleeting and of the moment
Words grow wings
Flying and out of the mouths of singers and crowds
But never caught fully
Never pinned down
Celebrated for their imperfections
Because they are a disappearing creation
They live entirely in the moment
A vibration, an exchange of energy
And that way things can be misheard . . .
Reinterpreted, you don't have to be seen
You can be so loud so visible and yet
Totally hidden
By a flock of notes fluttering, already dying,
Disguising the somewhat ordinary if anxious writer
With their shimmering glory and colour

My grandfather said I am
Like the monarch butterfly
That got lost
I flew from North America
In the eye of my mother . . .
Drawn to the churches, frescos
And old books of Europe
The new world too new
Back to grey stone and skies
Ancient scrolls, death and dust
Old death, not this fresh death
There in your hand
Glowing and
Relentless

AMERICAN MOTHER

Crafted from Renaissance stone
Mostly these days I write poetry on my phone.

I wish I had more of your staunch American character,
Strong, bold, and unflinching, like the desert, or a New York skyscraper.
But I am more like the English weather
Unpredictable and ever changing,
Prone to downpours.
Battered by sudden winds – thin-skinned, eye-bagged and always cold,
Proud and leaking.
Did you think you would give birth to such an English creature,
With your warm American blood.

I just found a picture of me
Drunk in a corridor with Liza Minnelli,
Waiting for Lady Gaga to go on stage.

I make songs to tie people to me,
With a ribbon of fantasy around their necks
Such a beautiful bow
That I hold in my fist.
And will not let go.

RAGE

I'm worried we are entering an age of rage,
Where only anger will be considered an asset
And the gentle will be mocked, then eaten.
Those with soft voices will have their tongues cut out,
As punishment for not using them the right way.
Don't you know your words are weapons,
Kindness is obsolete,
As obsolete as handwriting,
As obsolete as silence and darkness in a city.

OH YOU'RE A REAL MAN

Oh you're a real man
And you do what you can
You only take as much
As you can grab with two hands
With your big heart
You praise God above
How many have to die
So that you can feel loved.

OH AND YOUR

AND YOU DO WHAT

YOU ONLY TAKE

CAN ~~EH~~ ~~HAN~~ WIT

GRAB

WITH YOUR BI

PRAISE GOD AR

HOW MANY HA

SO THAT YOU C

REAL MAN

OU CAN

MUCH AS YOU

TWO HANDS

HEART YOU

VE

TO DIE

FEEL LOVED.

MONSTER

So you start to take pieces of your own life

And somewhat selfishly
Other people's lives
And feed them to the song
At what cost
This wondrous creature
That becomes more precious to you
Than the people that you took from

How awful

To make human sacrifices
A late night conversation
A private thought
All placed upon the altar

But you have to satisfy the monster
The monster has loved you for longer
Than anyone else.

TO DO
SLOW
MIRACLE
TO DO
WORLD WIDE
HEART BREAK
TOUR.
TO DO
FALSE GODS
NEW GODS
NO GODS
TO DO
Anti Fuck-boy
Magic Magic

I WOKE UP IN BED WITH
TWO ~~TEN~~ ~~TEEA~~ TEENAGE
VAMPIRES
I DONT THINK THEY HAD
EVEN ASKED ME IN.
I DONT KNOW HOW I HAD
ENDED UP SLEEPING
SWEETLY BETWEEN THEM
NEIL WAS BANGING ON
THE DOOR
WITH SOME CLOTHES FOR ME
MY DRESS HAD BEEN
SHREDDED IN THE NIGHT
NOT BY THE VAMPIRES
THOUGH, THERE ARE
OTHER THINGS THAT BITE.

I LIKE PEOPLE WHO'VE SEEN SOME DARKNESS

I like people who've seen some darkness
The haunted ones.

I like people who don't claim to know what love is
The honest ones.

LOCHGILPHEAD

My record for drunk dialling someone was forty-seven times in a row
I then ended up on a flight to Glasgow,
And a four-hour coach journey
through my Scottish grandmother's childhood holiday destinations,
Which is a pretty strange way
To try and keep the party going.
My father was quite taken by the romance of the situation,
Totally unplanned . . .
He thought somewhere in my grasping desperation,
falling through churchyard hedges and climbing out of club windows in town . . .
I had set off an internal satnav
Leading me to retrace her footsteps . . .
A rest stop at Lochgilphead,
which I remember as being incredibly beautiful,
I may have been hallucinating,
but I think there was a carousel
I sent apology texts.
In a floral nightie
Almost passing for a dress.

MY MIND HAS CLAWS
AND SETS OF TEETH
IF LEFT UNCHECKED
IT WILL EAT AND EAT

DEPRESSIVE
PACKMAN

MAYBE IT WOULD BE FUN

You appear like a mirage on a New York street, hungover and striding towards me.
How is it that you have kidnapped me fully, fully, fully

God help me
I wish that you could stay
And I could stroke the pain away
use my body as a bandage
I tell myself I'm not like that any more
At least I thought I was less savage
I try, I try, I try, I try, I try to do less damage

And so my head is turned again
By someone breaking before me,
They see I'm cracked too
So they cannot ignore me
Of course you would adore me
And maybe it would be fun
Before you totally destroyed me.
Oh you're just like my father,
And his father before him,
Drunk and charming and writhing in your own skin

LOVE HOSPITAL

Remember the twenty-four hours that we checked in
because we were both sick,
And we tried to nurse each other
in the way that drowning men drag their rescuers down with them.
We were both kicking and screaming
in a quiet way, with fever and hallucinations
and we kept taking the medicine.
That only made it worse

DOOMED SHIP OF YOUTH

WEDDING

London is a graveyard of ex-boyfriends
Family trauma
And scenes that smashed themselves to pieces

I've been going out among the ghosts
Hurting, hunting

Dancing so I don't have to speak,
Bringing bodies close to me
But going home alone

I have kissed almost everyone at this wedding

In the doomed ship of youth
I am lost
I am still in love with all of you
So I try to stay away

I am trying to keep you safe

HONEYMOON

All the people I have savaged
Held in my mouth

Shook 'em out

They rattle behind me
As I enter the room
Such jagged music

Like tin cans
On a honeymoon

the tenderest emptiness

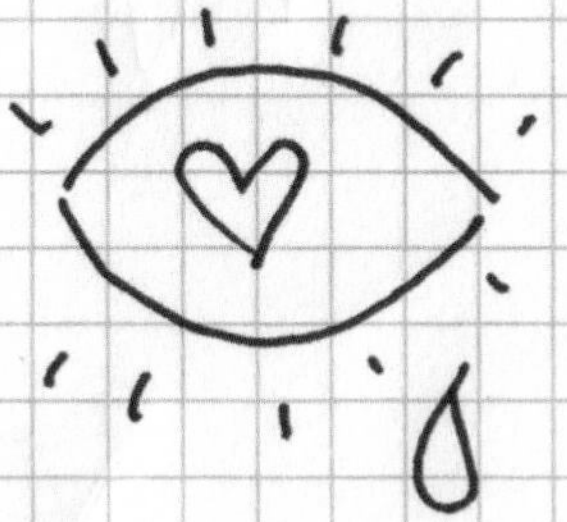

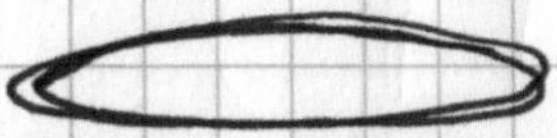

DOOM PORTAL

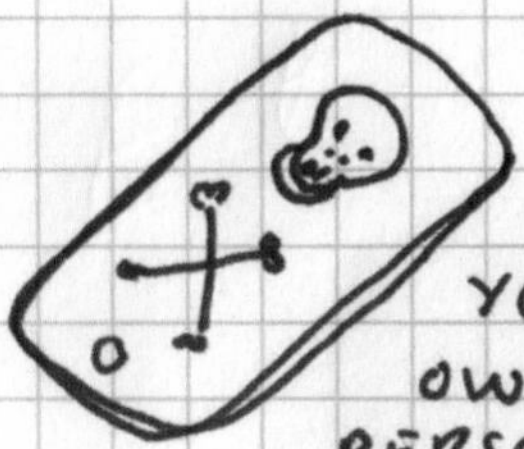

YOUR OWN PERSONAL SAD MACHINE

I GUESS I WON'T WRITE POETRY

I guess I won't write poetry
I'll just stare at my phone for fucking eternity

The blank face of god
Your demon door
Your own personal sad machine

I rode my bike over the bridge

In a shoal of other cyclists
Like shimmering fish

The passing buses
Become enormous groaning whales
Maybe this human mess is not so bad
I put my despair on hold

Being 'Famous'
Is like being an anxious ghost
Scared to scare people
Wanting to slip through unseen
But somehow keep your shape
People scream when they see you
You are an apparition
A figment of your own imagination
Are you?
Are you?
Am I?
Fuck I don't know

GOD IS NOT IN

YOUR PHONE.

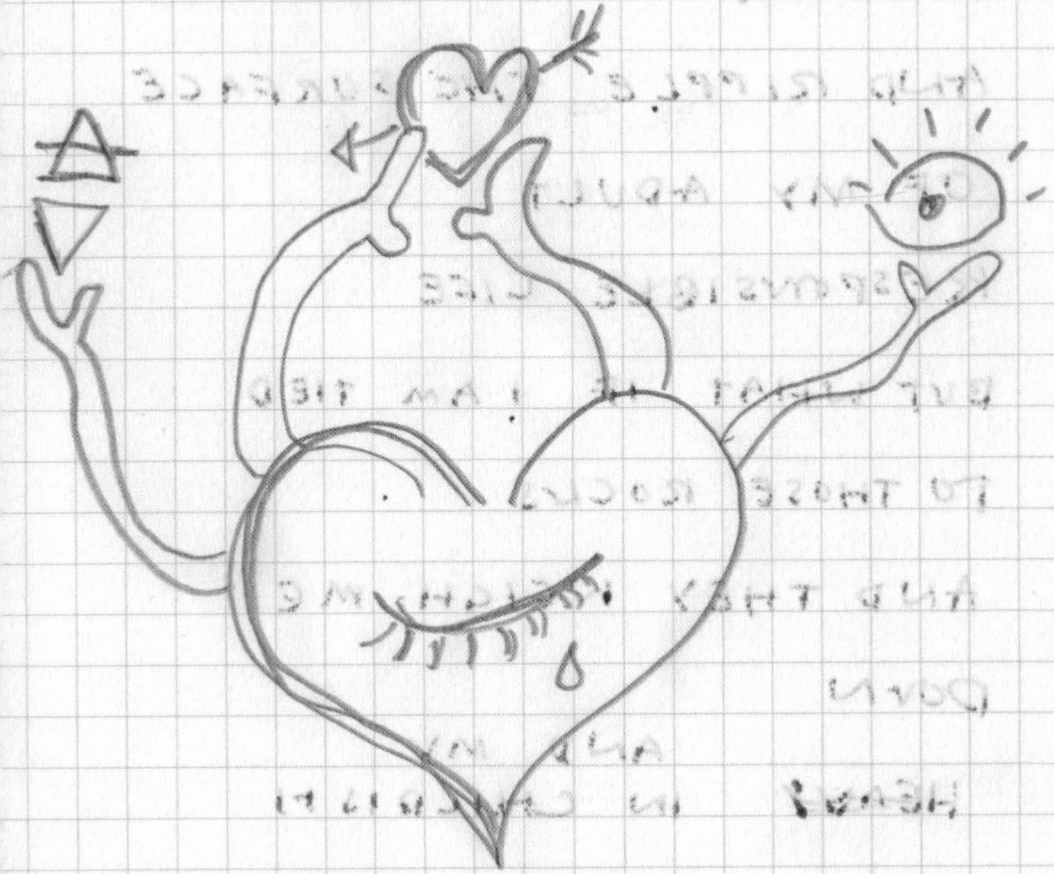

I GUESS I WONT WRITE

POETRY, I'LL JUST STARE

AT MY PHONE FOR

FUCKING ETERNITY.

SONG

The song speaks in grand prophecies
Older and wiser than me
Trying to out-think death and out-swim the sea
What would I say
If it was just me
Not full of choirs, singing fucking constantly
How would I speak
If the song left me
That strange knowing entity
Man nor woman
Genderless, luminous,
And free
Left me as it found me
Hollowed out.
Self-absorbed
Checking my phone and watching TV

I CANNOT WRITE ABOUT THIS

I cannot write about this,
It is a wordless thing

When did you become something
I couldn't write about,
Did you become real to me?

Now it is altogether
Too grown up
Too sad
Too 'the best for us both'

To put into poetry

Dr
Tea

THANKS

I would like to thank Robert Montgomery for giving me the idea to write poems in the first place, and for finding the title; as always my manager, Hannah Giannoulis; Nick Cave for his inspiration and encouragement (and a few bits of editing!); Yrsa Daley-Ward for her influence, support, and for setting the bar so high; my editor, Juliet Annan, for getting me to do this and for putting up with my anxious emails; Gill Heeley for all her amazing creativity; Tom Beard for making the swamp so beautiful; Between Two Books for being such a bright spot in my life; my father for his keen eye, and for instilling me with a love of poetry; all the people I have written songs with and all the people I have written songs about.

FLORENCE

INDEX OF TITLES

INDEX OF FIRST LINES

IMAGE CREDITS

The publisher is grateful for permission to reproduce the images on the following pages. Every effort has been made to contact all copyright holders. The publisher will be happy to make good in future editions any errors of omission or commission brought to their attention.

Cover artwork © Florence Welch.

Photos and postcards on pp. 9, 17, 33, 34, 99, 123, 156, 174, 180, 199, 215, 221, 231, 235, 253 and 279 courtesy of the author.

Photography on pp. 64–5, 91, 130, 151, 175, 208 and 262 © Tom Beard/Prettybird.

Marbling on pp. 39, 52–3, 94–5, 122, 182, 192–3, 209 and 268 © Jemma Lewis Marbling & Design.

p. 2: William Morris (1834–96), *Gold and red sunflower* wallpaper design, 1879 (colour woodblock print on paper), Private Collection/Bridgeman Images.

p. 8: William Morris (1834–96), *Snakeshead*, 1876 (block printed cotton) © Victoria and Albert Museum, London.

p. 10: Illustration created using William Kilburn (1745–1818), Textile Design, *c.* 1788–92 (w/c on paper)/The Stapleton Collection/Bridgeman Images.

p. 18: Artist Unknown, *Narcissus, c.* 1500 (wool and silk), Museum of Fine Arts, Boston, Massachusetts, USA/Bridgeman Images.

p. 25: William Morris (1834–96), Design for *Vine* wallpaper, *c.* 1872 (w/c on paper), Private Collection/Bridgeman Images.

p. 33: William Morris (1834–96), *Wallpaper with acanthus leaves and wild roses on a crimson background*, Private Collection/ Bridgeman Images.

p. 39: Jacob Chr. Roux, *Partial dissection of the chest of a man, with arteries indicated in red*, 1822 © Wellcome Collection.

p. 43: Edward Coley Burne-Jones (1833–98), *Hope*, (watercolour with bodycolour), Private Collection. Photo © Christie's Images/Bridgeman Images.

p. 56: (*border*) William Morris (1834–96), *Original drawing for a full-page border*, 1892–5 (ink and pencil). Photo © Christie's Images/Bridgeman Images.

p. 62: John William Waterhouse (1849–1917), *The Lady of Shalott*, 1888, Tate, London. Photo © akg-images/World History Archive.

p. 70: John William Waterhouse (1849–1917), *Ophelia*, 1894 (oil on canvas), Private Collection. Photo © Christie's Images/Bridgeman Images.

p. 74: Walter Crane (1845–1915), *Wallpaper showing a design of pine-needles and cones* (detail) © Victoria and Albert Museum, London.

p. 77: Sandro Botticelli (Alessandro Filipepi), *The Virgin Adoring the Sleeping Christ Child*, National Galleries of Scotland. Purchased with the aid of the Heritage Lottery Fund, the Art Fund, the Scottish Executive, the Bank of Scotland, the Royal Bank of Scotland, Sir Tom Farmer, the Dunard Fund, Mr and Mrs Kenneth Woodcock (donation made through the American Friends of the National Galleries of Scotland) and private donations, 1999.

p. 79: William Morris (1834–96), *Design for tapestry* (w/c on paper), Private Collection/Bridgeman Images.

p. 80: Nicolas Hilliard (1547–1619), *Queen Elizabeth I, 'The Ermine Portrait'*, 1585 (oil on panel), Hatfield House, Hertfordshire, UK/Bridgeman Images.

p. 84: Manuel de Arellano (Mexico, 1662–1722), *Virgin of Guadalupe (La Virgen de Guadalupe)*, 1691 (oil on canvas). Purchased with funds provided by the Bernard and Edith Lewin Collection of Mexican Art Deaccession Fund (M.2009.61). Photo © Museum Associates/ LACMA.

p. 90: Tamara De Lempika (1898–1980), *Portrait of Madame M*, 1932 (oil on canvas), (detail), Private Collection/Bridgeman Images © Tamara Art Heritage/ ADAGP, Paris and DACS London, 2018.

p. 95: George Charles Beresford (1864–1938), *Virginia Woolf*, 1902 (b/w photo), National Portrait Gallery, London.

p. 99: (*pattern*) Artist Unknown, *Floral design of Roses and Lilacs*, c. 1850 (glazed and roller-printed cotton) © Victoria and Albert Museum, London.

p. 103: Gustav Klimnt (1862–1918), *The Kiss*, 1907–1908 (oil on canvas) (detail of 601), Osterreichische Galerie Belvedere, Vienna, Austria/Bridgeman Images.

p. 110: Gustav Klimt (1862–1918), *Minerva* or *Pallas Athena*, 1898 (oil on canvas), (detail), Wien Museum Karlsplatz, Vienna, Austria/Bridgeman Images.

p. 114: Peter Paul Rubens (1577–1640), *Portrait of Marchesa Maria Serra Pallavicino* (*c.* 1575–*c.* 1630), 1606 (oil on canvas), (detail), Kingston Lacy, Dorset, UK. Photo © National Trust Photographic Library/Derrick E. Witty/Bridgeman Images.

p. 118: Gustav Klimnt (1862–1918), *Detail of Water Serpents I*, 1904–1907 (oil on canvas), Osterreichische Galerie Belvedere, Vienna, Austria/Bridgeman Images.

p. 131: Tamara De Lempika (1898–1980), *Portrait of Ira P*, 1930 (oil on panel), (detail), Private Collection/Photo via Christie's Images/Bridgeman Images © Tamara Art Heritage/ADAGP, Paris and DACS London, 2018.

p. 132: © Martyn Thompson/Trunk Archive.

p. 134: Artist Unknown, *A Shipwreck*, 1850, Universal History Archive/UIG/ Bridgeman Images.

p. 138: © David Mushegain/Trunk Archive.

p. 142: Jules Charles Ernest Billaudot, aka Mage Edmond (1829–81), *'Oracle' Tarot Card of Love, c.* 1845 (cardboard and gouache), Paris, France. PVDE/ Bridgeman Images.

p. 143: Ferdinand Victor Eugène Delacroix, (1798–1863), *The Virgin of the Sacred Heart*, 1821 (oil on canvas), Ajaccio Cathedral, Ajaccio, Corsica/Bridgeman Images.

pp. 144–5: © Colin Michael Simmons/Gallery Stock.

p. 148: Eujarim Photography/Getty Images.

p. 150: Gran Cenote, Mexico © Ismael Eduardo P.M. via Flickr.

p. 157: (*pattern*) Hartmann et Fils, *Flowers of India on a Trunk, c.* 1800 (printed cotton), Munster, Germany © Victoria and Albert Museum, London; (*painting*) Niccolò de Simone, (1636–77), *Saint Agatha,* c. *17th* (oil on canvas). Photo © Christie's Images/Bridgeman Images.

p. 162: © Marlene Marino/Trunk Archive.

p. 163: Jack Pierson, *One More Lie Hollywood Told Me, c.* 1990 © Jack Pierson, courtesy Cheim & Read, New York.

p. 170: © Nancy Jo Iacoi/Gallery Stock.

p. 176: © Tamara Lichtenstein.

p. 184: Vali Myers (1930–2003), *Foxy*, 1967, (pen, black ink and watercolour), 34 x 23 cm. Image provided courtesy of The Vali Myers Art Gallery Trust and Outre Gallery, www.outregallery.com.

p. 194: William Morris (1834–96), *Utecht Velvet*, 1871, Private Collection/The Stapleton Collection/Bridgeman Images.

p. 199: (*pattern*) Artist Unknown, *Dress fabric with floral pattern*, late eighteenth century (cotton), France © Victoria and Albert Museum, London.

p. 202: Cy Twombly (1929–2011), *Fifty Days at Iliam: Shades of Eternal Night*, 1978 (oil, oil crayon and graphite on canvas), Philadelphia Museum of Art, Pennsylvania, PA, USA. Gift (exchange) of Samuel S. White 3rd and Vera White, 1989. Photo via Bridgeman Images. © Fondazione Nicola Del Roscio.

p. 204: Nicolas Robert (1614–85), *Frontispiece of 'La Guirlande de Julie'*, *c.* 1642 (w/c on vellum), Private Collection/Bridgeman Images.

p. 221: Pompeo Batoni (1708–87), *Sacred Heart*, Rome, Church of the Gesu. Photo © Scala, Florence/Fondo Edifici di Culto – Min. dell'Interno.

p. 222: Patti Smith at Hotel Chelsea, New York City, May 7th, 1971 © David Gahr/Getty Images.

p. 224: Cy Twombly (1929–2011), *Tulips (IIII)*, 1985 (polaroid), Rome © Fondazione Nicola Del Roscio.

p. 232: Antique Map of London © Liszt Collection/Bridgeman Images.

p. 243: Cy Twombly (1929–2011), *The Rose (IV)*, 2008 (acrylic on plywood, panel: 99 13⁄16 × 72 13⁄16 inches), (detail), © Cy Twombly Foundation. Courtesy Gagosian.

p. 244: William Morris (1834–96), *Anemone* design (textile), Private Collection/ Bridgeman Images.

pp. 249 and 263 © Quentin de Briey.

All other images courtesy of the author.

Published in the United States by Crown Archetype,
an imprint of the Crown Publishing Group, a division of
Penguin Random House LLC, New York. Originally published
in hardcover by Fig Tree, an imprint of Penguin General,
a division of Penguin Random House Ltd., London, in 2018.
crownpublishing.com

Crown Archetype and colophon is a registered trademark
of Penguin Random House LLC.

The image credits on pages 284–287 constitute an extension
of this copyright page.

Library of Congress Cataloging-in-Publication Data is available.

ISBN 978-0-525-57715-7
Ebook ISBN 978-0-525-57716-4

PRINTED IN CHINA

10 9 8 7 6 5 4

First American Edition

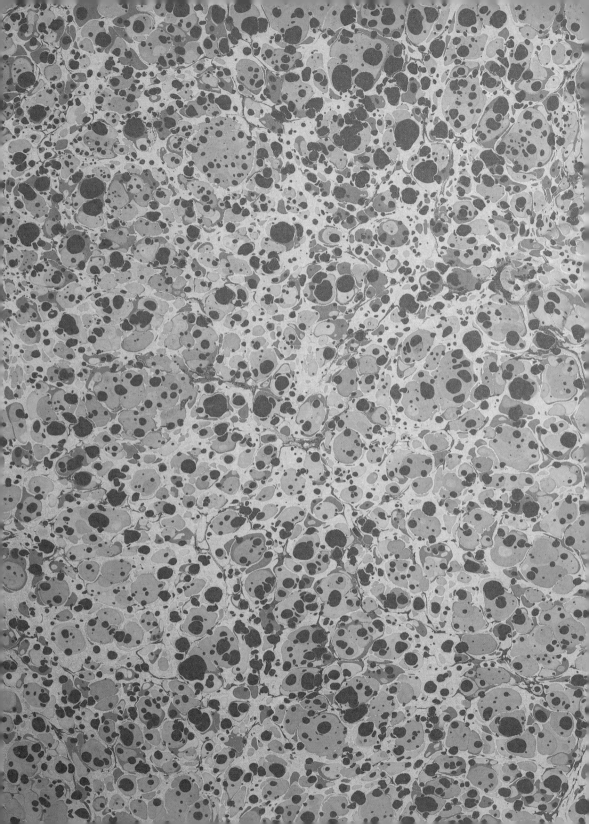